Mastering People Management

Build a successful team –
motivate, empower and lead people

Mark Thomas

THOROGOOD

Reprinted by Thorogood 2003
10-12 Rivington Street, London EC2A 3DU

Telephone: 020 7749 4748
Fax: 020 7729 6110
Email: info@thorogood.ws
Web: www.thorogood.ws

A catalogue record for this book is available from the British Library

ISBN 1-85418-096-7

Printed in India by Replika Press

...nagement

er and lead people

Mark Thomas
BSc(Econ), DipPm, FIPD

Mark Thomas is a Director of Performance Dynamics, an international business consultancy specialising in change management. Prior to Performance Dynamics he worked with Price Waterhouse Management Consultants where he advised on the organisation issues arising out of strategic change. His business experience encompasses mergers and acquisitions, privatisations and major restructuring initiatives. He currently manages a wide range of client assignments from business planning facilitation and organisation reviews through the process re-engineering, organisational surveys and executive development initiatives.

Mark is a Fellow of the UK Institute of Personnel and Development. Previously he held a range of management roles in the information technology and food industries where his experience involved all aspects of organisation development and human resource management.

Mark's current work focuses on strategic change management and people development. He facilitates business planning and top team events and runs a wide range of organisation transformation programmes: which include process re-engineering and internal consultancy. He works throughout Europe, Australia and the Far East and is a frequent conference speaker and writer on organisation and human resource issues; having contributed to a number of books on organisation change. He was also previously Programme Director for Management Centre Europe's Strategic Human Resource Management Programme and is currently Programme Director for a leading UK Mini MBA Seminar. Mark was also involved in running some of the first public, Business Process Re-engineering programmes in Europe and Australia. Mark's experience covers financial services, telecommunications, manufacturing, transport, information technology and local and central government. His clients include many major international and multi-national corporations.

Contents

Icons

Throughout the Masters in Management series of books you will see references and symbols in the margins. These are designed for ease of use and quick reference directing you quickly to key features of the text. The symbols used include:

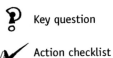 Key question

 Guide to best practice

Action checklist

 Key learning point

 Activity

Key management concept

We would encourage you to use this book as a workbook, writing notes and comments in the margin as they occur. In this way we hope that you will benefit from the practical guidance and advice which this book provides.

What is management?

....

Chapter 1

Understanding management

About five months ago Jean Simons gained a promotion to a managerial role. She had been a top class information systems designer and was excited about the opportunity to manage other people. Within two months of her appointment her team of six programmers and two designers were experiencing all sorts of problems. Jean attributed these difficulties to her clients' changing demands but her team blamed it on her inadequate people management skills.

As managers the skills we use on a daily basis are a central feature of our lives, yet many of us spend little time trying to review or develop our management practices and processes. Today many of us have dual roles involving technical tasks and people management . We have to sell, generate business or fix problems as well as look after other people. In some cases the demands are immense. Yet day to day pressures frequently mean we have little time to stand back and analyse what it is we are doing as managers. The result is that we drift along and so run the risk of developing bad habits and practices. In today's hostile corporate world this is a dangerous mistake. We need to be constantly identifying new ways of managing and continually updating our skills so that we stay sharp.

The effectiveness of the people who work for us is often determined as much by our ability in managing them as their individual competence. In turn our success is often determined by the way we are managed by our boss and whether we have sufficient autonomy, responsibility and support or guidance. So our management effectiveness is largely determined by our ability to manage people relationships and to achieve results through them.

While working with people demands an integration of technical expertise and interpersonal skills, dramatic changes in technology are forcing even more radical changes in organisation structures and methods. As a consequence traditional approaches to managing are under review. Authority in today's organisation is not automatically given to someone because of their position in the hierarchy. Knowledge and expertise are gaining greater currency at the expense of older styles of management which have paid deference to rank and authority. People no longer expect or are prepared to carry out tasks simply because they are told to do so by a manager. People want to know the 'why' of an action as well as the 'what'. No longer can any manager in any organisation anywhere be sure that their past management performance will guarantee future success.

In order to succeed in today's fast changing organisation managers need to demonstrate new ways of influencing, persuading and achieving commitment and co-operation. At the same time they need to be ever open and willing to listen to other people's ideas. We might argue that this is not a new notion – managers have always had to be good listeners. But the need for higher levels of interpersonal skills are more critical than ever. Faced with extreme levels of global competition all organisations need to innovate and challenge more than ever. The uncertainty facing organisations is greater than it has ever been and the need for people working in organisations to share ideas and challenge each other is a pre-requisite for survival when faced with complex problems and opportunities. This requires managers and their people to be comfortable in having their ideas not only listened to, but also constructively criticised, without taking offense or feeling that their authority or expertise has been called into question. In many organisations this is not as easy as it might first sound.

Many organisation cultures actively discourage the effective challenge of their managers ways and ideas. Many managers are deeply uncomfortable at the thought of having their ideas challenged or critiqued by junior staff. To do so in some organisations is to jeopardise your career path or continued development! But this has to change. The vast majority of managers in organisations are still unable to sit down in front of their people and give negative feedback in a positive and constructive manner! Until we have addressed this challenge we can forget fanciful ideas about becoming team based and learning organisations. So mastering people skills is now a big issue for all managers!

When analysing our own people skills we need to recognise that we have all learnt from our own experiences to behave in particular ways. Some of us are aggressive and demanding, pushing to get our way at all costs. This for some people can lead to a domineering or autocratic style of management. Other people are more placid when it comes to dealing with people at work; perhaps too inclined to let others have their own way at the expense of some specific organisational goal. This manager is often and rather unfairly characterised as a 'soft touch'. Of course neither of these styles is right. Aggressive and bullying managers often get their due rewards even though it may be a long time in coming. While the more easy going manager may lose out on opportunities because they may be felt to lack the killer instinct needed to survive in a hostile and competitive corporate world.

This view was identified as far back as the late 1950's and 1960's when two highly influential models were developed which characterised these management styles. In 1958 R Tannenbaum and WH Schmidt wrote an article in the Harvard Business Review entitled 'How to choose a leadership pattern'. This characterised the classic management styles and was again very significant in shaping managers' thinking.

Key Management Concept

Tannerbaum and Schmidt
How to choose a
leadership pattern
Harvard Business Review,
1958

Continuum of leadership behaviour

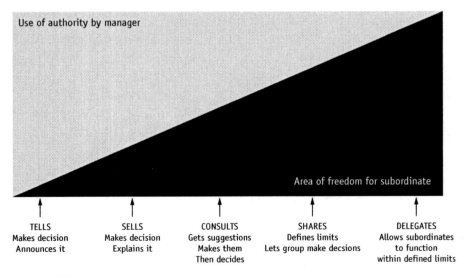

Use of authority by manager

Area of freedom for subordinate

TELLS	SELLS	CONSULTS	SHARES	DELEGATES
Makes decision	Makes decision	Gets suggestions	Defines limits	Allows subordinates
Announces it	Explains it	Makes them	Lets group make decsions	to function
		Then decides		within defined limits

Tannenbaum & Schmidt, Harvard Business School

Then in the late 1960's R Blake and J Mouton, two American psychologists, developed their equally famous grid which characterised the task and people continuum facing managers.

Blake/Mouton managerial grid

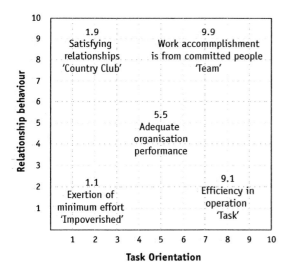

In the Blake and Mouton model managers were characterised by their focus on the task at the exclusion of people – the so called 9.1 manager, or the people manager who focuses only on satisfying relationships – the 1.9 "Country Club" manager. Their model suggested that the ideal was a 9.9 manager who combined a high task and productivity focus with high levels of people support and enthusiasm.

What all managers need to do is develop a flexible range of styles to deal with different types of people in different situations, and we will shortly examine some models that help us to do that.

So what is management really all about?

The need for management arises when a group of people tackle a task that is too large or complex for any one individual to cope with. When faced with such situations people soon discover that they need to define tasks and allocate roles in order to develop a solution. The process of breaking tasks or problems down into key elements has traditionally involved the classic management practices of Planning, Organising, Staffing, Directing, Co-ordinating, Reporting and Budgeting; – or the acronism POSDCoRB as they have come to be known. These activities make up the essential elements of most traditional management roles and they can be defined as the classic functions of management.

The classic functions of management

The planning function

Planning involves establishing in broad outline the main objectives and tasks that need to be achieved and the organisation methods for accomplishing them. Planning is intended to provide a strong focus for any project or task. It comprises the following elements:

Forecasting

Estimating your organisation's future needs and requirements. For example, market share, profit and revenue streams, return on investment.

Establishing objectives

Establishing the outputs or results that have to be achieved. For example, increase production, sales, profitability by x%. Increase customer response times by y.

Scheduling

Establishing the priorities and a sequence of actions to achieve the objectives. What is the order in which things need to happen?

Budgeting

Allocating the resources necessary – people, equipment and finance – to achieve the objectives. For example, a financial budget of $1.5 million and a project team of 10 people supported by 3 contract workers.

Establishing procedures

Developing and applying standardised methods and processes for conducting the work. For example, what project management or process control systems will we use?

The organising function

These activities involve establishing the formal structures of authority so that the various tasks and activities can be defined and co-ordinated amongst the people involved. It also includes the selection and training of people to deliver the necessary results.

Selecting people

Identifying the right people with the appropriate skills for the tasks or roles to be performed.

Delegating

Allocating the necessary levels of responsibility, authority and accountability to people to complete the work.

Establishing working relationships

Creating the right atmosphere and climate for effective team working and the development of strong and productive working relationships.

The directing function

These activities involve getting people to take action and comprises the following elements:

Decision making

Arriving at the right findings, conclusions and recommendations, and making appropriate decisions in a timely manner. 'Following the detailed presentation we now need to decide whether we commit to the next phase of the project today.'

Communicating

Creating a shared understanding of the goals and objectives through the use of a range of effective communications channels. 'We want to be number one in all our principal markets.'

Motivating people

Energising people and encouraging them to deliver high levels of performance. Maintaining a strong willingness to deliver at all times regardless of temporary setbacks and disappointments.

Developing people

Guiding and advising people on how best they can develop skills and capabilities so as to increase their value and realise their full potential.

The controlling function

This function involves monitoring any work in progress so as to deliver results. It involves recording and inspecting projects or work plans and establishing any financial planning, accounting and controlling procedures. The function also involves advising and reporting to senior managers on progress.

Establishing performance standards

Establishing the criteria by which work processes and results will be assessed and measured.

Measuring performance

Recording and reporting on work in progress to see if it is meeting the required quality and performance levels.

Evaluating performance

Evaluating and appraising the work and results achieved.

Correcting performance

Taking timely and corrective action to improve working methods and performance results.

The POSCoRB model of management has had a huge influence on management thinking and has resulted in many of today's standard management practices. The manager as a controller and director of people and resources has been applied in most organisations for the last few decades.

But things are changing

Whilst these models have had a huge impact in shaping the way we think about management, there is now a major shift away from some of the central foundations of this traditional management thinking. Intense global competition and new technologies are providing constant and complex new challenges to those who seek to build and sustain leadership positions. Organisations are having to address the following challenges with new perspectives and principles of organisation:

- **Fast responses**: how do we reduce the time delay between identifying and satisfying market needs?

- **Continuous innovation**: what does it take to ensure that we continue to bring new ideas, products and services to market faster and more cost effectively than the competition?

- **Customer satisfaction**: what does it take to get close to the customer and to deliver customer satisfaction at the right cost?

These challenges are forcing many organisations to radically rethink the role of management. Faced with the need to do more and more with less and less the traditional perspective of management as a controlling and directing function is under review. Many of the world's leading organisations are actively exploring the notion of people becoming self-directed. Words such as empowerment, which involve individuals being entrusted to get on with their jobs without reference to management are now common place and have major implications for traditional managerial roles.

The basis of this new thinking is that it is no longer viable for organisations to have lots of management layers and roles involved in simply checking and controlling other people. If your organisation is facing immense challenges from high quality and low cost competitors and you have too many managers performing little 'value added' roles then you will lose.

Managing in the knowledge era

Many organisations have now begun to redefine their expectations from management. The emphasis today is on people becoming self-directed and taking greater responsibility for their day to day actions. This recognises the essential shift that is taking place in the world of work, whereby traditional notions of what constitutes value in the organisation, such as capital and plant, are rapidly if not already being replaced by the notion of **intellectual capital** which places a higher premium on people's skills, imagination and capabilities as a source of competitive advantage. Such change demands a very different concept of managing whereby the manager assumes the role of coach and facilitator. Enabling takes the place of checking and controlling.

New organisation structures are demanding more people capability

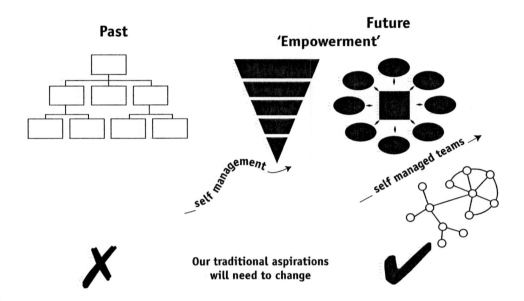

The fundamental question in this process of transition is a simple one: 'if we have the right people with the right skills and motivation, then why do we need people wandering around and checking on them?' This belief in empowering people to take responsibility for their actions is likely to accelerate in the face of global markets and competition.

The new management model is based on the following dimensions:

- **A high level of interpersonal skills and the ability to communicate, motivate and mobilise people towards particular and shared goals.**

- **The ability to create a positive working climate so that people feel free to challenge and communicate their concerns and ideas.**

- Involving people in decision making processes so that they are able to contribute to key processes and enjoy enhanced levels of commitment to the aims and objectives of the organisation.

The process of managing in the knowledge era also requires a greater degree of conceptual thinking in order to work on strategic activities. Today's manager needs to deal with abstract concepts more than ever and must be able to view the organisation as a total system rather than through a narrow functional perspective of finance, information technology or production. This ability to think and use conceptual skills is critical as they enable managers to rise above day to day operational thinking and view the wider corporate and business environment. Indeed whilst many managers have traditionally lost out in later stages of their career development if they were judged to be lacking in a strategic thinking perspective, such skills now apply to almost any executive in any organisation regardless of position.

In the knowledge era the emphasis for managers is on thinking not doing – this is a challenge for many of us!

Key Learning Point

Adapting the process of managing for the knowledge era

To understand management in the knowledge era is to view it as a dynamic process that consists of four critical stages; setting direction; empowering; enabling, and reviewing.

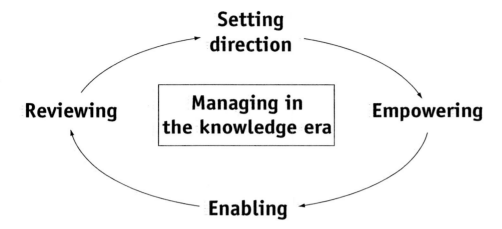

These four stages can be described as follows.

Setting direction

This involves the notion of setting the direction and involving people so as to secure agreement to the key goals and objectives. Drawn from the classic POSCoRB model this retains the essential elements of clarifying and agreeing the results that are to be achieved. Providing focus and vision for people is the key.

Empowering

Empowerment has become one of the great buzz words of 1990's corporate life. But few people understand what it means. Essentially it is not about giving people freedom to do absolutely anything but rather a means of establishing and agreeing very clearly what has to be done, by what time and by whom in order to achieve the planned results. So empowerment involves establishing clear boundaries of responsibility and accountability.

Mark Brown has developed an elegant model to clarify a complex area. He argues that managers simply need to be clear with their people on the following areas:

A model for empowerment

Source: Mark Brown

- **No Go.** These are areas that staff have no responsibility or involvement with – they are the strict domain of the manager.

- **Know Go.** These are areas or issues where, providing the manager has been consulted and given authority, the person can act.

- **Go Know.** This involves issues whereby someone can act but they have to keep their manager advised of what they have done.

- **Go.** This is the field in which people can act without any reference to their manager.

Enabling

This process involves ensuring that people have the necessary resources and capability to deliver the agreed results. It necessitates cultivating the right conditions to enable people to perform. Freeing people from needless interference or obstructions in order to deliver results. It also involves communicating fully to people who may be involved in the performance process.

Reviewing

Reviewing performance and taking corrective action where needed is the final stage in our performance cycle. The reviewing process also involves improving performance by identifying and taking advantage of new opportunities. This is not simply checking up on people but rather an exploration with people to see if the best possible results have been achieved and to examine what can be learnt from the experience. Critical in this whole scenario is the importance of people skills. The need for managers to become people management experts.

Management in this model is very different to the emphasis placed on direct control and direction that we observed in the classic POSCoRB. Under the empowerment model managers are required to provide the necessary conditions for people to flourish under their own energies. The focus is on cultivating a clear and guiding sense of individual worth, responsibility and commitment, as opposed to a dependency culture where the individual is unable to function without a manager directing proceedings. Of course broad direction still exists but the focus is on the individual becoming self directed. The manager's role becomes that of coach.

Two classic approaches to managing and leading that can help us manage in today's organisation

Faced with these rapid changes there is no need to re-invent the wheel as there are two classic models that I believe are as useful today as they were when they were first developed some twenty years ago. John Adair's *Task Team and Individual Model* and Paul Hersey and Ken Blanchard's *Situational Leadership Matrix* are famous for helping managers think about their individual style and have been applied in many organisations. I believe that the focus both models place on managers learning to delegate and trust other people is as valid to the new challenges facing management as they were when first developed. The problem is that sometimes in organisations we are so busy chasing the latest thinking or fad that we forget what has already been developed, and both of these models help managers understand the dynamics involved in 'letting people go' to develop their real capabilities – the challenge in leading today's organisations.

Key Management Concept

Action-centred leadership

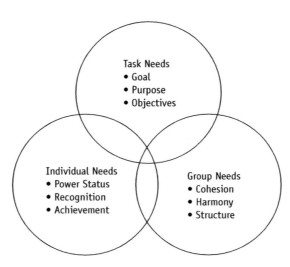

Task Needs
- Goal
- Purpose
- Objectives

Individual Needs
- Power Status
- Recognition
- Achievement

Group Needs
- Cohesion
- Harmony
- Structure

In a distinguished lifetime of studying leadership John Adair describes leadership as the act of balancing three critical dimensions at the same time. These dimensions relate to the emphasis any leader places on :

- Achieving the task or goals.   *Task*

- Developing individuals and their capabilities.   *Individual*

- Building a team out of a group of individuals.   *Team*

The essence of Adair's approach is that these three dimensions must be managed if we are to be effective. Success cannot be achieved in isolation – well developed individuals need to work well together as part of a team. Similarly teams are not effective if they don't achieve their goals and complete tasks on time. If a leader neglects one of these three areas it will impact on the others. For example, a team that is not focused will result in poor working relationships and their ability to complete the task.

Adair's ideas on leadership can be summarised as follows:

Action-centred leadership – a checklist

Action Checklist

- Define the fundamental mission and objectives of the team: 'Why do we exist?' Providing a sense of purpose and direction.

- Communicate the goals with enthusiasm and focus people on their key task(s).

- Work in teams of four to fifteen people and help people understand the three elements of Task, Team, Individual.

- Design and agree clear roles for people. Communicate those roles.

- Ensure the continuing commitment of individuals to the team.

- Replan when necessary and check on progress with the team.

- Set individual targets after discussion and consultation; discuss progress with each team member.

- Delegate decisions where ever possible to encourage responsibility and accountability.

- Consult with people on important issues or decisions.

- Communicate the importance of everyone's role.

- Brief your team regularly on developments – successes, problems, people and other points of action.

- Train and develop people constantly.

- Care for the well-being of team members; constantly seek to improve working arrangements.

- Deal with grievances promptly.

- Monitor progress; learn from successes and mistakes; practice Managing By Wandering Around (MBWA), observe, listen and praise.

- Have fun!

Checklist: Leadership The John Adair Model

	Key Functions	Task	Team	Individual	Action-centred Leadership
Communication	Define Objectives	Identify task and constraints	Involve team Share commitment	Clarify aims Gain acceptance	
	Plan Organise	Establish priorities Check resources Decide	Consult Agree standards Structure	Assess skills Establish targets Delegate	
	Inform Confirm	Brief group and check understanding	Answer questions Obtain feedback Encourage ideas and actions	Advise Listen Enthuse	
	Support Monitor	Report progress Maintain standards Descipline	Develop suggestions Co-ordinate Reconcile conflict	Assist/ Reassure Recognise effort Counsel	
	Evaluate	Summarise progress Review objectives Replan if necessary	Recognise success Learn from failure	Assess performance Appraise Guide and train	

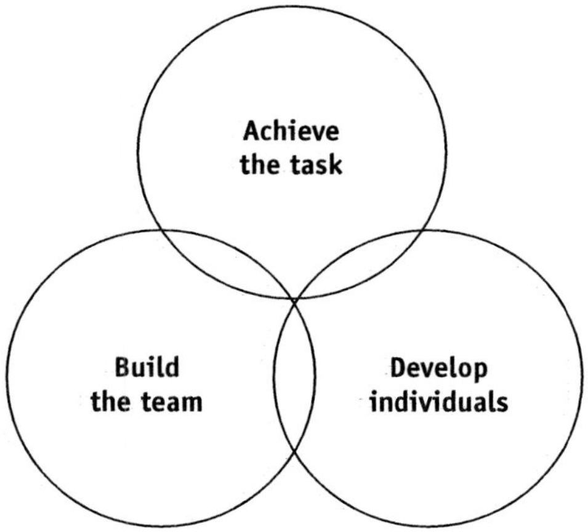

Task, team & individual model

1
Achieve tasks

- define goals & tasks
- check resources available
- set standards of performance

2
Build the team

- share responsibility
- consult with people
- encourage people

3
Develop individuals

- delegate tasks and responsibility
- encourage people
- promote trust and integrity

- brief people
- check people's understanding
- manage time pressures
- manage stress
- recognise priorities
- be decisive
- monitor and report on progress
- review objectives

- respond to questions
- look for and give feedback
- co-ordinate people
- manage conflicts
- recognise successes
- encourage creative and innovative approaches
- take risks
- use humour
- learn from successes and failures
- have fun

- recognise hard work and commitment
- appraise and reward understanding
- train people to develop and fulfil their potential
- listen to people all the time
- counsel people

Key Management Concept

Situational leadership

Paul Hersey worked with Ken Blanchard (of 'The One Minute Manager' book fame) to produce the highly influential *Situational Leadership Matrix*. Their main contribution to the study and understanding of leadership and management was to break the myth that there is an ideal leadership style for all situations. Rather (as is in the model depicted below) managers and leaders need to adapt their leadership style to different situations.

Hersey and Blanchard argue that two major factors affect an individual's response to a leader:

- ***The emphasis we place on the task being carried out***. The more we stress the task the more directive our behaviour will need to be. In other words the more we will specify what we want, when we want it done, and the manner in which it should be completed. When we are highly task focused as managers we are very specific and leave the person having to do the work little if any discretion as to how they might complete the task.

- ***The emphasis we place on our relationship with staff***. The more we stress this factor, the more supportive our leadership and management behaviour will be. When we are in a highly supportive mode we will encourage and praise good work and seek to develop strong and close working relationships.

Hersey and Blanchard illustrated the relationship between these two factors in the form of a matrix comprising four different leadership styles.

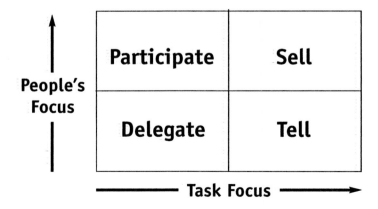

Leadership: the most valuable attributes of a leader

Telling style • high task – low relationship

- The manager who uses this style effectively controls the work of staff closely and acts quickly to correct and redirect shortfalls in performance. They make sure staff are clear about what they have to do. They will also emphasise the use of standard procedures and stress the importance of targets and deadlines, for example:

  Let me be clear as to what I want you to do.
  I will explain precisely how the work must be completed.
  You then need to ensure that you have contacted x. Do you fully understand what I am asking you to do?

Selling style • high task – high relationship

- The manager who uses this style effectively shows concern for the task as well as staff relationships. They spend time in friendly conversation, but make sure staff are clear about their responsibilities and the required standards of performance. They incorporate and support but retain overall control about how a task is completed.

  This is a great opportunity for you so let me explain what we need to do....

  Thanks for coming in today I am pleased to be able to get you involved in this project as I think you can learn a lot from it. So let me outline what you need to do.

Participating style • low task – high relationship

- The manager who uses this style effectively lets staff organise and manage their own work following consultation. Managers who are participative do not lead in a directive manner but rather allow individuals to set their own goals. Participating style managers also encourage and support positive contributions.

- They will be available for discussion and advice , but will not push this involvement. They try to minimise direction and endeavour to make staff feel important and involved. Staff will be allowed to determine their own roles and priorities with guidance being available if requested.

  So I have outlined the situation, what are your ideas as to how we might approach the customer?

  So what do you think?

  I would be very interested to hear your comments.

Delegating style • low task – low relationship

- The manager who uses this style effectively delegates and lets staff define problems and formulate solutions by themselves. They do not intervene with people unless they are specifically requested to or unless their monitoring processes lead them to think there may be a problem- in which case they will switch to a participating style of management:

  So over to you.

  I guess you can get on with that without help from me.

  Here's a new assignment for you to carry out.

It is now generally accepted that there is no such thing as a 'best' style, only the 'best' style in any given situation.

Situational leadership argues that in order to be effective managers we need to adapt our style, according to the maturity of our people to carry out the task they are working on. Hersey and Blanchard define maturity from two fundamental aspects:

- **Motivation.** Is the individual motivated and willing to do the work?

- **Competence.** Is the individual competent to do the work? Do they have the necessary level of skills, and experience?

Based on our answers to these questions an effective manager decides the best style to use in any given situation. Situational leadership suggests applying the four classic styles:

The telling style

- Where people have low levels of competence and low levels of motivation this indicates that close supervision from a manager is required, as otherwise the work may not be completed. For example, with new staff it is essential that close attention is paid to clarifying their roles, responsibilities and limits of discretion. Attempts to use participating or selling styles are less effective because whilst good relationships may be established, people still need to have a clear understanding of their job and what is expected of them.

The selling style

- If a manager continued to be totally directive and used a telling style all the time people would become resentful and demoralised. In some cases they would be unwilling to assume or take on further responsibility. So as someone matures in a role an effective manager will want to encourage the individual by becoming more supportive. Conversely, if someone still lacks competence the manager cannot rely on the individual completing the task well. So they still have to be task focused but combine it with a high level of relationship support to encourage and respond to someone's enthusiasm. Equally for a manager to jump to a participating style of managing would fail because the individual involved is still not competent to make their own decisions without clear guidance.

The participating style

- As people become increasingly competent and motivated, an effective manager no longer needs to emphasise the importance of the task and can instead concentrate on establishing closer working relationships. This relationship enables a manger to keep in touch with the individual and their work and, if necessary, make it easy to move back to a selling style to correct any problems. A prime benefit for the manager in moving into a participating and delegating style is that they are far less time consuming management styles. Thus they should start releasing the manager to do other work.

The delegating style

- When a high level of staff maturity is reached by an individual – namely when someone is highly skilled and motivated- a manager can in effect delegate and withdraw leaving the individual to get on with it. This also has the effect of providing additional motivation through the delegation of additional responsibility.

In general, if there are performance problems, a manager can move back to a different style – from participating to selling. Equally, if an individual's performance is good, a manager can advance – from telling to participating. Throughout any management process consistency is important, as too many style changes create confusion and uncertainty. The worst managers of all are those who continually jump from one style to another. They often move from Participating to Telling and back again. Not surprisingly, such managers complain frequently about the unwillingness of their staff to assume responsibility, whilst staff complain about being confused and de-motivated.

Management style is a complex and difficult area. Few managers get it right. Situational leadership however, provides a straightforward way of assessing individuals and situations and deciding successful management styles.

Situational leadership • four styles summary

•	Telling	Highly directive and for individuals who are either:
		1 New to their work and need to be supervised.
		2 Will not perform the task unless directed to do so – namely unwilling people.
•	Selling	Very directive and supportive for individuals who do not yet have the necessary level of capability but who do need their confidence developed and encouraged.
•	Participating	For individuals who can succeed but who may need some support to build their confidence and motivation.
		To find out any problems – Why is someone who is able not keen to do something?
•	Delegating	For highly skilled, competent and motivated individuals who know what they are doing!

Activity

"A"

Assess your leadership style

Two leadership behaviours

- Directive   Giving individuals clear instructions about how, when and where they do things.
- Supportive   Listening and encouraging people. Getting their involvement and commitment .

But will managers become extinct?

Many people are naturally disturbed by any discussion that raises the basic worth and value of managers. Indeed some managers become concerned that their jobs are being threatened and that managerial jobs are facing extinction. Of course the truth is probably somewhere in between. What is clear is that there will always be a need for managers who are involved in setting direction and shaping the future of organisations. At the same time in large enterprises there will also be the need for these managers to be supported in carrying out similar activities at an operational level.

Equally it would seem to be clear that there will be less need for the numbers of managers that we have had in organisations in the past. Today's communications and information technology are enabling organisations to radically rethink their structures such that technology can enable people to do a lot more in terms of tasks that would previously have been carried out by managers.

The key questions for any future manager in any organisation would seem to be the following:

Are you placing too much emphasis on securing a management role? – after all it is only a title.

What you do besides telling people what to do? How do you add real value to the organisation?

If you lost your management role tomorrow what would you do? What could you do?

Key Question

In the future other skills such as technical, market, customer or information technology skills may serve us better than our sole ability to manage. Remember roles are only the function of how organisations have decided to operate – your customer does not care about that detail, they only want the right product or service at the right price.

So what is the new management skill set?

It seems clear that managers in the future will be judged more on their ability to motivate people than has been the case in the past. Of course the need to deliver results will remain but indications are that managers will need to deliver on both measures – results and people. Managers who achieve results at the expense of people will be marginalised.

Managers wanting to use the Adair and Hersey, Blanchard models will need to get into the Individual, Team and Delegating spheres of activity. Encouraging people to become self sufficient and to work under their own powers of motivation will be the guiding force. Listening and putting people at the centre of competitive activity will become critical management endeavours. This will require managers who are comfortable in operating without the trappings of existing organisation life. People skills are in!

Leadership: the most valuable attributes of a leader

1	Ability to take decisions	14	Capacity to speak lucidly
2	Leadership	15	Astuteness
3	Integrity	16	Ability to administer efficiently
4	Enthusiasm	17	Open-mindedness
5	Imagination	18	Ability to 'stick to it '
6	Willingness to work hard	19	Willingness to work long hours
7	Analytical thinking	20	Ambition
8	Understanding of others	21	Single-mindedness
9	Ability to spot others	22	Capacity for lucid writing
10	Ability to meet unpleasant situations	23	Curiosity
11	Ability to adapt quickly to change	24	Skill with numbers
12	Willingness to take risks	25	Capacity for abstract thought
13	Enterprise		

(Rank order of attributes cited most frequently by a cross-section of successful Chief Executives)

Source: Management Centre Europe Survey

The need to develop new and radical approaches to managing is not borne out of a sense of well-being towards people. It is a case of economic survival! The fact is if I can operate with two layers of management and you need five I will kill you on costs. Plus I will get my new products and services into the market place faster. Whereas you have to get them through all that bureaucracy, game playing and politics. So good luck and watch out that the competition don't innovate you out of existence.

Key Learning Point

Characteristics of the knowledge era and the worst of old world managers

The Knowledge Era managers are:

- Interested in your role
- Supportive and excellent listeners
- Aware of your role and capability
- Not interfering
- Decisive
- Enthusiastic
- Flexible and willing to change
- Available to their people
- Able to set clear objectives
- Results focused
- Open-minded
- Willing to develop and grow people
- Able to develop high levels of trust
- Good at letting go
- Strong communicators
- Sincere – they never tell lies
- Approachable
- Keen to hear your views and ideas
- Balanced in their moods and disposition
- Consistent and positive in their actions
- Self-motivated – this 'rubs off' on people
- Interested in your opinions and views

Old World managers are:

- Ineffective communicators
- Disrespectful of other people's time
- Bad listeners
- Indecisive
- Always changing their minds
- Suspicious of their staff
- Not interested in developing their people
- Keen to blame others
- Judgmental and temperamental
- Selfish
- Lacking in team / individual development
- Frequently defensive and insecure
- Dictatorial and autocratic
- Threatened by talent beneath them
- Always taking the credit for good work
- Unwilling to allow their people access to higher authorities
- Unprofessional
- Manipulative
- Bad at providing positive feedback
- Practitioners of public humiliations
- Inconsistent
- Rude and bullying

Warning – why managers have traditionally got fired in organisations!

- Never delivered results

- Lacked a sense of urgency

- Lacked a sense of priorities

- Were unable to respond positively to change

- Clinged to obsolete ideas and outmoded ways of doing things

- Useless at managing people

- Emotionally volatile and unstable

- Immature in their behaviour towards others

- Gave up learning and developing

- Were unable to delegate

- Ineffective communicator

- Unable to take tough decisions

- Lacked a sense of humour

- Lacked humility

- Failed to anticipate problems or challenges

- Focused more on 'I' rather than 'We'

Mastering yourself

· ·

Chapter 2

Getting in shape for the future

'Loyalty is a dead concept so start to get selfish'

As managers we have to clearly recognise – if we don't already know it, that we are living in very changing and challenging times and that the rate of change is continually accelerating. Security and comfort in our management roles is now a thing of the past. In today's knowledge era we must be totally focused on enhancing our own capability and market worth. This means we need a highly polished and prized set of up to date skills. Nowadays we never know when we might find ourselves in the wrong place at the wrong time. At the time of writing this book a debate is taking place in economic and management circles as to whether job insecurity is any greater in the 1990s than it was ten years ago. Some commentators argue that it is not and that the job insecurity issue has been exaggerated. They argue that the so called 'psychological contract' whereby employers and employees buy in to the notion of fair pay and rewards for a fair day's work is alive and well. But be it a hostile takeover or major downturn in market activity I would argue that no one is safe in corporate life and that the traditional contract is now void. The fact is that organisations always have and always will pursue their own aims and objectives, and in the majority of instances this necessitates individual needs taking a back seat. No matter how successful or secure an organisation is you can never be sure that some other organisation will not acquire you, dramatically enter and destabilise your market or simply innovate you out of existence. We therefore need to think not so much about our job security but rather our employability.

So I would argue that we have actually reached the stage where loyalty is an almost, if not already, outmoded concept for organisational and corporate life. There are no longer great prizes for staying with one employer for any great length of time as you leave yourself open to sudden changes which can catch you off guard. Moving from one employer to another used to be described as job hopping but today it is seen as a sign of someone who is taking care of their development. Of course there is nothing wrong with staying with one employer for a long time provided that you are growing and developing your skills and experience. The time to begin questioning this approach is when you sense that you are not developing.

So being selfish and managing your skill set and employability is a pre-requisite of survival in today's corporate environment. The corporate world has never been a bigger jungle than it is today and taking action so as not to become another corporate victim is essential. If you ignore the need to develop your skill set, then you have only yourself to blame if events catch you out. The fact is we all need to get selfish and start thinking about our personal development in a big way. Remember losing your job is no longer a capability issue – anyone can now find themselves in the wrong place at the wrong time. However, this is not meant to frighten but rather to alert people and provide a call to action. Although I suspect that for many people simply discussing this issue is deeply uncomfortable. But rather than avoid the issue we need to begin to get used to it and start to think about our skills and development as a long term investment. After all it is our own research and development base and if we neglect it our overall value and worth falls.

Insecurity as a daily phenomenon

Remember -The only difference between a rut and a grave is the depth!

For most of us taking direct control and responsibility for our development is not an easy process to start contemplating. Many of us work in large organisations because we perhaps feel we would be uncomfortable working in a smaller business or in a self-employed capacity. We perhaps feel that we need the stimulus of an office environment to keep us going or that we would just not feel comfortable trying to plough our own way. The result is that we have not really been forced to think of alternatives or what would happen if we lost all the comforts(or what little remains) of our immediate corporate life tomorrow. But the fact is, that we now have to do so, and we have not only to think about it but also be well prepared for it happening.

For those managers who want to start a process of continuous self improvement many have little idea about how to start structuring their development. If you have been working with one company for several years it is very easy to not only neglect your skills development, but also to forget how to market yourself. However, getting stuck in a rut and losing sight of some basic skills in self-marketing can be overcome with a little determination and planning.

A first starting point in beginning to enhance your market value as an executive is to develop a personal development plan that systematically sets targets and milestones to develop your skill set and capabilities.

Action plan

Activity

Getting in shape to deal with job insecurity – the first step – think the unthinkable – it could happen!

Take the first step and start thinking and discussing the employability issue. Ask yourself:

- What would you do if you lost your job tomorrow?
- How much shock would you be in?
- What would you immediately plan to do?
- Have you developed any contingencies?
- What would be your financial exposure? How long could you go before beginning to experience some discomfort?
- Do you have an up to date cv?
- What work or career avenues would be open to you?

The key point is to begin to confront the issue – to see it not as some traumatic event but as perhaps a normal feature of working in today's employment world. In many ways insecurity has always been there, it is just that in today's world it strikes without impunity and on a more widespread and frequent basis. The challenge therefore is to plan for it happening and not become a weak victim. Adopt a positive and aggressive approach to the challenge rather than a passive reactive one. The positive side of a more aggressive stance is that it also brings new opportunities and opens new doors.

Developing a personal development plan

A Personal Development Plan (PDP) prepares you to manage changes and challenges in your working life. The aim is to get you thinking in a structured way about your skills and market worth by committing to a process of continuous self improvement – thereby enhancing skills, experience and employability. This in turn will enable you to secure greater work satisfaction and employability. A PDP assists you in realising your full potential and worth.

Getting focused – setting some personal objectives

In many management roles once we have achieved a certain degree of success and some of life's other commitments come along, we soon start to forget about where it is we are going. In effect we settle into a steady routine – until of course that sudden crisis in the form of a merger or acquisition occurs and galvanises us into late but very serious action to protect our future, either inside or outside the organisation. A personal development plan forces us out of relaxed and complacent thinking and instead challenges us to develop new skills and capabilities.

The first step in any PDP involves setting some short, medium and long term goals with regard to our working and private lives. The purpose of any objective or goal setting is to get us focused on what we really want to achieve. Remember goals prevent us from drifting along. Goals help lift our thinking and provide a sharp focus for our day to day lives. The discipline of setting objectives and actually committing them to writing is a very powerful process. If we leave things to chance the chances are that we will be disappointed. The mere act of writing down our key goals can act as a constant and readily available reminder

Answering these questions will help you start to develop your own Personal Development Plan.

of our real intentions. Carrying these goals around with us and looking at them in either quiet or stressful moments can help refocus our energies and thoughts.

At the same time we will need to think about the 'how' part of achieving any objectives. So our starting point involves finding quality time to think about our goals and ambitions for both life and career.

We may need to reflect on the following questions:

- Am I happy with my present role?

- Do I enjoy my working environment?

- Am I gaining the right level of financial reward for my efforts?

- Am I continuing to learn and develop?

- Have I continually had new challenges presented to me?

- Do I like working with my boss, colleagues, customers?

- Have I the right balance between work and family?

- Does my role allow me the opportunity to pursue other interests outside of work? Or have I already sacrificed certain things?

- What do I like doing? (At work or play)

- Do I see an appropriate future beyond my existing role?

- Am I happy with any future developments as they appear?

- Is my current role stretching me as an individual?

- Am I satisfied with the investment being put into my development by myself and employer?

- Has my employer always delivered on promises?

Also in considering our work and personal goals we should ask ourselves what more do we want to achieve:

- A greater balance between career and home life?

- A more challenging working role?
- A better professional, academic or skills qualification?
- A change of organisation or work role?

Drawing a life line chart

A simple and powerful way to review your current situation and reflect on the future is to draw what is called a career or life line. All we have to do is draw a line which reflects our life or career to date on the diagram illustrated below.

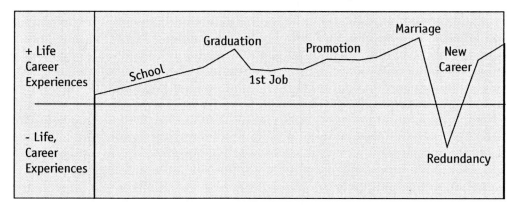

Anything above the line is a positive experience and below the line is regarded as a negative event. The height and depth of any points reflects your degree of delight or unhappiness with the event.

Begin the process by mapping out the big events in your life (school, sporting, academic success or failure, college, graduation, first jobs, marriage, children, divorce, career change, redundancy, promotion, birth, death of close ones etc)

Remember to leave space to fill in other events as certain events will trigger others.

Activity

Drawing your life line and reviewing these questions will help you to focus on the priorities to include in your Personal Development Plan.

Once you have drawn your line reflect on the events and ask yourself some of the following questions. Using different signs mark the events as you rate them:

- Which were the big positive experiences for me? Why were they so influential?

- What were the big lows? Why?

- From which experiences did I learn most?

- Where did feel best suited and fulfilled?

- Where was I most under pressure or stressed?

- Where did I have most or least control? How did I feel about that?

Then consider the major themes that emerge from your life and career to date:

Ask yourself what are the common themes about the way you do things and the roles you seek out.

- What do you seem to value or prize most?

- What do you not like doing?

Then consider your future.

- Where do you see yourself going in the future?

- What do you want to achieve?

- What would be your preferred role and personal circumstances?

- How is what you are doing today helping you to achieve what you really want?

Conducting a personal SWOT analysis

Another element to reviewing our goals is to drawn up a personal SWOT analysis.

Developing a personal SWOT analysis

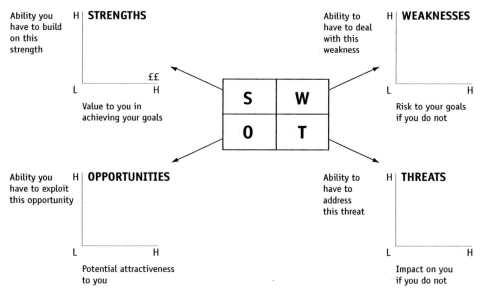

Think about your skills and capabilities
The opportunities you have available

This simple techniques asks us to list all our perceived strengths and weaknesses in terms of skills, attributes, interests, attitudes, likes and dislikes. At the same time we are asked to highlight any potential opportunities and threats that we may have to face. A SWOT analysis is very powerful for capturing on one sheet of paper our current circumstances. Once we have exhausted our analysis we can then reflect on some critical issues i.e. the things we really want to do or exploit as well as highlighting the things we want to avoid.

Activity

Draw up your own personal SWOT analysis.

Once we have reviewed our life/career line, developed a personal SWOT analysis and we are clear as to what we want to achieve, we can then start to set some objectives around our key goals. When we set any personal objectives or for that matter any other type of goal we always need to assess them against the acronym **SMART**: for any goal to be effective it must be:

Key Learning Point

Specific:	Goals should specify clear behaviour or actions.
Measurable:	Our goals should specify a basis for measurement so that we know when they have been achieved.
Achievable:	Goals should be within our capability to achieve.
Realistic:	Any goal needs to be stretching but at the same time realistic.
Timely:	Goals need to have a time element attached – when they will be achieved.

If any of our goals cannot be assessed against these five dimensions we should consider redrafting them. Whilst we can all easily set goals without a real sense of commitment to achieve them we need to remember that a personal development plan requires us to be disciplined. So we need to spend quality time to really focus on our key goals. We must be specific in terms of what we want to achieve and the timescales involved. We also need to ask ourselves if we are being unrealistic.

We should also consider who might help us in providing resources or encouragement to keep us track when we inevitably lose interest?

Key Question

The seven essential questions in your personal development plan

1 What new skills, capabilities or situations do you want to develop to enhance your value in your professional and/or personal life?

2   How do you intend to develop these skills and capabilities or engineer the right circumstances – what are your specific goals?

3   What key activities or decisions will you need to undertake and by when?

4   What support will you need to achieve your goals?

5   What other information, resources or support will you need?

6   What key activities will you undertake and by when?

7   How and when will you review your progress?

Getting support for your personal development plan

The mentoring role

Having decided to develop a PDP and having mapped out a realistic action plan, we need to put our plan into action. Of course it is up to us as to how we go about it – but remember unless we do something... nothing will happen!!! All too often we fall short of committing ourselves to specific objectives and as a result time drifts and we find ourselves achieving very little. As we have already stated, the process of committing ourselves to pen and paper in drafting individual goals can be very powerful. So don't just think about it, DO IT TODAY and commit your goals to paper! You will find that it does provide real focus and if you get into the habit of referring to them regularly they will help you stay focused and enable you to keep going even when you are feeling down.

Another means by which we can move forward on the personal development front is to make a contract with someone to help us over time. This does not need to be a formal or written arrangement but can be a simple verbal agreement with someone to act as a support or guiding source for your development plans.

This supporting or facilitating role is often referred to as a mentor and it could be performed either at work or outside by :

- A close colleague or friend.
- Your immediate manager.
- A group of colleagues.

A close colleague or friend

- This might be someone who has similar development plans or aspirations as yourself. By working together and providing support and helpful advice and encouragement to each other on a regular basis you can keep going when you might feel like giving up.

- When thinking about a mentor try to choose someone who:

  - already possesses some of the skills or capabilities you want to acquire so they can provide some form of help or advice immediately.

  - will commit fully to helping you with support and encouragement – you in turn must also be willing to offer similar assistance if requested.

  - you respect or admire in some way – someone who can be relied upon to listen at all times.

Your immediate manager

If we have a successful working relationship with our manager there is no reason why we should not use them as a mentor. Good managers always play a strong mentoring role. Of course there may be occasions when we might want to be discrete about revealing long term plans or ambitions. Only you can decide if you would feel comfortable in developing such a relationship. However, many of us might feel uncomfortable about talking about leaving our organisation for another opportunity. But certainly there are many managers who make great mentors and provide excellent support.

A group of colleagues

A small group of working colleagues can provide a wider network of support for carrying out the mentoring role, provided that everyone is fully committed to support each other. Clearly a group working in such a way requires a strong sense of mutual respect and support. But with the right people we can do much to support each other and develop strong mutual co-operation.

Whatever form of mentoring you select, you MUST commit to regularly review your development plan with your mentor. It is no use carrying out reviews in a haphazard manner. We must be disciplined to ensure that we are achieving the targets we have set ourselves.

Eight key activities to assist us in developing our skills portfolio

1. Self-directed reading

Self directed reading involves developing our skills and knowledge through a programme of selected and targeted reading. To secure maximum benefit from any such programme we need to focus on the specific range and depth of information that we need to improve our knowledge or skill base. When developing a programme of directed reading that we should consider the following sources as they can provide significant information for development and knowledge:

- Internal notes and minutes from meetings.

- Internal reports and documents.

- In-house publications.

Activity

Developing your skills portfolio.

- Professional journals.

- Books.

- Newspapers, magazines and periodicals.

Action Checklist

Techniques for self-directed reading.

Action points

- Be aggressive in making notes in the margin of books or underlining sections in articles. Use highlighter pens as well to indicate important points or passages.

- If you see a good article in a newspaper or magazine cut it out to read at a later date.

- Operate a binder where you put things to read in quiet periods. If you don't you won't do it.

2. Secondments

Secondments are concentrated periods of time spent in other departments or functions within your organisation. The aim of a secondment is to help us understand how other parts of the organisation operate. At the same time a secondment might take place with a customer or supplier to help us understand different businesses practices and approaches. If your business does not operate such a policy why not ask or request that you spend some time working with another department, customer or supplier.

To achieve real benefit from any secondment establish:

- Clear objectives for the secondment period. What is it that we want to learn or develop?

- An agreed and structured programme of work – leaving things to the person we are allocated to is not advisable. So agree a set of clear learning objectives.

- A date for a structured review and follow up afterwards.

3. Training and development programmes

Formal training and development programmes, when selected and matched to our learning needs, can provide an excellent and accelerated means of improving our skills and capabilities. When considering any training or development programme as part of our development ask the following questions:

- What knowledge or skills do I want to improve or develop?

- Is a training programme the most effective way of meeting my needs? Can I gain the skills or knowledge by any other means?

- What courses are appropriate and available to obtain that knowledge or skill?

- What is the reputation of the course or provider?

- How will I evaluate the learning?

- What is it I want to emerge from the training being able to do?

4. Videos

Another relatively easy and low cost option to develop our knowledge and skills are training and business videos. They offer a flexible resource which we can use in our own time. Today a vast array of videos covering almost every skill area exist. From interviewing skills to business and marketing strategies we can be sure that a video exists. Some organisations have developed their own video libraries with a view that people can help themselves and run the programme in their own time.

When using any video programme be sure to use any booklet which accompanies the programme to maximise the learning benefit.

5. Shadowing

Shadowing involves spending a period of time closely observing or accompanying people as they conduct their roles on a day to day basis. It might be regarded as similar to a secondment, but is generally more intensive and involves spending a shorter period of time.

The aim of shadowing is to gain an understanding of a particular role or operating environment. Again to secure maximum benefit from such an experience the person we shadow needs to have a clear understanding of what we want to achieve. At the same time they obviously need to be receptive to sharing information and insights on their role and work with us. Spending a day with a Sales Representative or Engineer operating with customers in the market place can provide a valuable and interesting experience.

6. Coaching

Our everyday work provides valuable learning opportunities. Indeed most of us actually learn most by working on the job. We can seek to maximise these learning opportunities through a structured process of coaching and guidance by selected managers. A coaching manager can provide extremely valuable sources of advice and guidance on a continuing basis.

7. Projects and assignments

Work projects and assignments can be powerful tools for learning and development, providing opportunities for developing our skills in a number of key management activities including:

- Project design and management.

- Information gathering techniques.

- Interviewing skills.

- Problem solving skills.

- Analysis of information and generation of proposals.

- Report writing.

- Presentations.

As well as increasing our knowledge and skills, special projects or assignments also provide us with new information and insights on our organisation. The important point with this approach is that any project needs to involve a real and live business issue. That way it will generate real management interest and so force us to generate a quality result. Irrelevant projects which do not enjoy management interest are unlikely to motivate us to deliver superior results or outputs.

8. Open learning

Open learning is a process involving the acquisition of knowledge and skills at a pace and place determined by you and involving a range of learning media. It is an approach that has and will continue to grow very rapidly with the onset of new and more exciting forms of electronic media.

At the moment flexible learning revolves around one or more of the following medium or methods:

- Specially developed work books.

- Interactive videos.

- Manuals.

- Audio tapes.

- Computer based learning – CD ROM's.

- The internet.

- Company IntraNets.

Clearly many people are predicting an explosion in opportunities via the Internet and in company IntraNets which will enable people to download training and learning packages onto their work or home computers. The effect will be to make learning much more accessible by distributing training and learning packages on a much more flexible and fluid scale.

Action Checklist

Getting balanced – how to start taking control and managing yourself and your true value

1 Keep focused on your key goals. Don't be distracted from achieving the things that really matter to you.

2 Work smarter rather than harder. Don't confuse long hours with effectiveness or efficiency. Moving paper around does not create value.

3 Avoid the use of negative internal dialogues such 'I can't..' and 'Yes, But!!!' Stop saying 'I will try!' Instead say 'I will' – we often defeat ourselves before we begin.

4 Avoid using words and expressions such as 'ought' and 'should have'. Instead use the words 'I could have' and 'I had the choice.'

5 Make sure you are achieving the right balance between your personal and work life.

6 Develop your ability to manage stress. If necessary attend a training programme or read a book on stress management. Be clear as to what triggers stress in your role.

7 For each trigger develop coping strategies to manage them. Always:

- Stand back from the situation and find time to gather your thoughts

- Change or avoid the stressful situations

- Change your response to the trigger 'I will no longer allow myself to react in that way!'

- Change your working hours – begin work earlier and finish earlier

- Vary your breaks

- Stay fit by exercising regularly – twenty minutes a day is all it takes.

8 Avoid work becoming a routine or chore.

9 Learn to relax and take time out for yourself. Reward yourself and do something that you enjoy – playing sport or some other hobby.

10 Keep a record of all your regular tasks. Prioritise the tasks that are critical. Ask yourself whether you are getting the best results in these areas? Stay focused on the vital few and not do everything.

11 Review the decisions you make over a couple of weeks and analyse how much time you devote to each one. Are you spending sufficient time on the important things?

12 When making decisions ask yourself either the cost of getting it wrong or the benefit of getting it right. Allocate sufficient time based on your answer.

13 Operate a mental 'development diary'. At the end of each day ask yourself:

- What did you learn today?

- What have you done that was new?

- What have you accomplished?

- What must you do tomorrow?

14 Say NO to people who place unreasonable demands on you.

15 Make telephone calls rather than spend time writing long memos and letters.

16 Try to reduce the length of all your written communications – letters, minutes, memos, e-mails, reports, instructions by 50%.

17 Seek out opportunities to make presentations and develop your skills in this area.

18 Ask close friends to give you real feedback on your performance during meetings, presentations etc.

19 In preparing for a difficult interview, presentation or negotiation, practice the session or role play it with a close colleague. Get their reactions to your proposed approach.

20 After attending any training programme make sure you review your notes within a week of your return, make a record of any points that you regard as especially important and that you will apply in your organisation. Produce a short report for your manager – better still make a presentation to the management team on some recommendations that the business should consider taking.

Activity

A

Assess your management skills.

Personal development questionnaire

This questionnaire is designed to help you start thinking about your personal development at work. It highlights some of the classic skill areas in managing and leading people.

- Review the list of skills below and decide which of the areas are important to your personal development.

- As the list of skills and competences is not meant to be exhaustive you should add others if you feel they are appropriate.

- At the end of the questionnaire identify the critical areas that you need to develop and consider some plans for developing those skills.

General management skills and competences	I'm doing OK	I need to do more	I need to do less
1 Thinking before I speak			
2 Communicating effectively with my team			
3 Being brief and concise when communicating			
4 Putting forward my points of view to others			
5 Making presentations to a group or team			
6 Developing other people's contributions			
7 Reading the organisation's politics			
8 Being assertive with others			
9 Really listening to people			
10 Contributing fully at meetings			
11 Using effective writing skills			
12 Understanding team dynamics			
13 Recognising conflicts in my team			
14 Recognising who needs support in the team			
15 Spotting potential in others			
16 Being ruthless in dealing with paperwork			
17 Managing my time effectively			
18 Planning my day at the beginning			
19 Being attentive to detail			
20 Being creative and innovative			
21 Seeking out more challenges and responsibility			
22 Focusing on my priorities			

General management skills & competences	I'm doing OK	I need to do more	I need to do less
23 Preventing interruptions to my work plans			
24 Delegating unimportant and non-urgent issues			
25 Finding time to reflect on the 'big picture'			
26 Understanding other people's role(s)			
27 Developing strong team spirit			
28 Showing interest in other people's needs			
29 Displaying trust in others			
30 Motivating others			
31 Challenging people's idea and assumptions			
32 Giving positive feedback and recognition			
33 Coaching, training and developing individuals			
34 Establishing in my team an atmosphere of trust			
35 Leading my team in an effective style			
36 Encouraging team involvement in decision making			
37 Communicating to others what I want			
38 Understanding and managing change			
39 Helping to sell changes			
40 Recognising when people are under stress			
41 Managing others who are under pressure			
42 Disagreeing openly with others			
43 Encouraging others to challenge my ideas			
44 Highlighting problems or challenges in plans or proposals			

General management skills & competences	I'm doing OK	I need to do more	I need to do less
45 Trusting others to do things			
46 Being a genuine coach to my people			
47 Assessing risk			
48 Managing stress and being relaxed when under pressure			
49 Dealing with conflicts			
50 Resolving differences between others			
51 Dealing with a lack of co-operation from others			
52 Facing up to disappointments			
53 Being comfortable with asking for help when I need it			
54 Handling difficult clients/customers			
55 Meeting with customers and clients			
56 Offering advice on training and career development to my people			
57 Understanding other people's values			
58 Keeping up to date with the latest developments in my field of expertise			
59 Understanding our management information systems			
60 Increasing my understanding and use of Information Technology			
61 Understanding and managing my responsibilities in disciplinary and grievance procedures			

General management skills & competences	I'm doing OK	I need to do more	I need to do less
62 Asking for feedback on my performance			
63 Asking for ideas/opinions from my peers			
64 Analysing problems and their real causes			
65 Confronting problems in the organisation			
66 Understanding the needs of other units that I have to work with			
67 Identifying and managing my career options			

Activity

Identify areas for development at work

List here the skills and competences that you think you need to be developing as a priority. What plans can you make to ensure that you will begin to acquire these skills?

Try to be specific and commit to some real actions with time scales.

Skills & competences I want to develop

```
1
Time scale:



```

```
2
Time scale:



```

```
3
Time scale:



```

4
Time scale:

5
Time scale:

6
Time scale:

7
Time scale:

8
Time scale:

Mastering performance management

Chapter 3

Managing performance

All of us want more than money from our work. We want roles that are interesting, challenging and developmental. Most of us also want to participate in the process of setting and agreeing our work objectives. These are essential elements to working in an empowered culture and working environment. And enhancing people's sense of satisfaction and growth in their work have now become priorities for today's manager.

Any process of managing performance must involve us as managers in a continuous and ongoing discussion with every member of our team. This process, which is often called Performance Management, is a structured means of ensuring that we and our people get the important things done. It is a way of clarifying:

- What your organisation and people expect from everyone who contributes to the organisation's overall goals and performance.

- Respective roles as managers and team members in working together and our ability as managers to provide effective direction, support and feedback.

- The training and development needs of your people.

Action Checklist

Things to avoid in implementing any performance management process

Many organisations have introduced performance management processes or systems. Whilst many work well, a lot more fall into disrepair . Listed below are some of the most common pitfalls to avoid:

- **An over reliance on procedures and paper** – do not allow your system to become too complex. Lengthy forms and numerous 'signing off' procedures do not encourage managers to use any system. Try to restrict any documentation to no more than two pages and keep your overall approach simple.

- **Poorly trained managers** – conducting a structured and professional discussion about performance requires critical skills in listening and giving feedback. Make sure you and your fellow managers are trained. There is a big difference between giving advice and counselling people! Managers need to be trained in how to get the best from any performance review.

- **Poorly defined targets** – Any performance management process must result in the development and agreement of objectives and targets. If the process cannot deliver in this vital area then it fails.

- **Lack of management commitment** – If the process does not enjoy the full support of management then it will be seen as a passing fad and managers will relegate it down their list of priorities. Make sure your system has the full visible support of senior management. Try stopping bonuses or pay rises unless all performance management discussions have been effectively carried out.

Motivating people at work also involves improving the team's performance, and any performance management process must be applied on a consistent basis across all team members to gain maximum benefit. A typical process for managing performance is illustrated below. In our earlier management model of empowering, enabling and reviewing we referred to this type of approach. It highlights the essential elements of managing performance that managers need to follow.

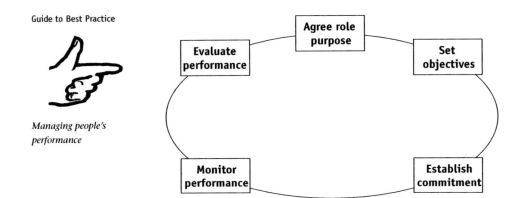

Managing people's performance

Agreeing the purpose of the role

In determining someone's role and their objectives, it is critical that both a manager and their people understand and agree their roles. This agreed definition and purpose can only be achieved by a focused discussion. People have to know why their role exists and what its purpose is.

Following an understanding of their role everyone then needs to know what performance targets are actually expected of them. At the same time most people will want to have a discussion about any goals that they are being asked to deliver. Some organisations focus on what are called the KRAs or Key Result Areas. These spell out the actual results that need to be achieved by the individual.

Setting individual objectives and establishing commitment

By demonstrating confidence in people and involving them in establishing their own objectives, they are more likely to be committed to achieving them. The words you use as a manager are the most powerful resources you have in terms of developing confidence in your people. In agreeing performance standards and KRAs managers will need to employ some critical inter-personal skills to successfully coach performance. These skills encompass:

- Active listening.

- Questioning.

- Giving and receiving feedback – both positive and negative.

What is an objective?

An objective is a statement of what tasks have to be completed and the measures by which the task will be judged to have been accomplished. An objective therefore makes a statement of

- What someone needs to do.

- Why they need to do it.

- How they will be measured.

How to develop effective objectives

Guide to Best Practice

Develop effective objectives

Use action words

Make sure your objective includes a precise and appropriate action verb to articulate what the person has to do: for example construct, develop, produce, analyse, detect, reduce, complete, deliver, prepare.

When setting objectives

In setting objectives ask yourself two questions:

How competent is the individual?

How committed is the individual?

Your responses to these two questions will provide you with a quick overview as to what you need to do in terms of providing the right amount of direction and control to the person you are managing:

- **Competent and committed people are self motivated.** These people will want to be stretched. They will respond well to being empowered and react favourably towards being set challenging and demanding targets and objectives.

- **Committed but not yet competent (still learning).** These people will need to be stretched but not excessively as their lack of competence means you will need to supply an appropriate level of coaching support and guidance. Setting unrealistic targets with this individual can destroy their developing confidence.

- **Competent but not committed.** If someone is not committed to their role but are felt to be competent in carrying it out you need to find out what the problem is. This is a case for a counselling discussion. It could be that the person is bored and no longer stimulated by the role. Either way you need to find out what their thinking is as they are obviously capable of greater performance.

- **Incompetent and uncommitted.** A problem individual which again requires a concerted approach to initially find out what the problem is. You will need to identify whether it is a training, personal or role issue or some combination of all three. This type of individual can absorb a lot of management time and so you really need to act quickly and decisively.

Be output focused

Make sure that any objective is stated in a way that emphasises the outputs. Remember the output may be a specific result, service, behaviour, product or interaction with someone. For example, an increase in sales of 10% by the third quarter or a reduction in customer response times from 30 to 15 minutes within the next two months.

Use performance indicators

A performance indicator indicates how someone will know that they have achieved the objective(s). Performance indicators often refer to:

- Time ('by when' criteria).

- Quantity (how many will be produced, sold delivered, saved, transferred).

- Quality (the level of satisfaction to be reached or attained).

When developing any objectives we also need to focus on some additional questions:

- What levels of desired performance can be achieved?

- Is the person or team working as effectively as possible in order to achieve these objectives?

- Are there other ways by which we can improve performance?

Action point

When writing objectives use action verbs to emphasise the output elements of your objective setting process. They help to provide a bias towards action and again focus people's thoughts and energies. For example: update; develop; introduce; deliver; reorganise; promote; build; set up; achieve; increase; generate; expand; reduce.

Activity

The need to 'build-in' performance standards

Some objectives may have an implicit performance standard built into the activity. For example, to increase the sales of product x by 25% by the quarter end. In activities where it is not readily apparent what the performance standard or outcome is you must build in a clear performance standard to avoid ambiguity.

For example, ***to regularly update the customer database.***
Such an objective as written remains loose and would benefit by the addition of more specific performance indicators. So it could be rewritten to include the following:
To update the customer database by 3.30pm Friday of each week and to transfer that data onto the main company database at each month end.

Monitoring performance

In order for anyone to understand how they are performing in a role managers have to provide timely feedback on performance. Any feedback we provide must be based on the agreed objectives and performance standards. Only by regularly monitoring our people's performance can we measure their effectiveness. This practice also provides a framework for discussing strengths and weaknesses in relation to the results you hope to achieve. By using regular reviews we can motivate our teams to gradually increase performance and to encourage people to monitor their own performance.

Warning: whilst performance can improve as a result of aggressive behaviour such as threats and intimidation, performance improvement is only ever likely to be short-term. Bullying managers who impose unrealistic objectives will invariably come up losers – even if takes a rather long time.

Evaluating performance

Evaluating performance is a critical element of any performance management process. Without it the whole cycle collapses. Evaluating performance allows you to check the endeavours of your team members and to reward high performance. As well as also dealing with poor performance it also helps you to identify any factors that may have been outside of someone's control and so adversely affected their results.

The evaluation process also enables you to reset the goals and so resume the performance management process.

What are Key Results Areas – KRAs?

There are generally four types of KRA:

1 **Operational KRAs** – these consist of the essential role performance indicators. The factors that you must deliver on.

2 **Projects** – these are specific 'one off' pieces of work that have predetermined outcomes that you have been asked to deliver.

3 **Personal development** – these are the targets that you set yourself as part of your ongoing responsibility for self development.

4 **People development** – these are the targets that you set to deliver the required levels of performance amongst your staff.

Objective setting checklist

Action Checklist

		YES	NO
1	I regularly discuss and agree objectives and KRAs with my people.	☐	☐
2	I hold regular (monthly) performance discussions.	☐	☐
3	I focus on a maximum of six key objectives.	☐	☐
4	Clear performance measures are always agreed.	☐	☐
5	Any objectives that are set are realistic and achievable.	☐	☐
6	Any objectives are agreed through discussion rather than management dictate.	☐	☐
7	We revise objectives in the light of any major external changes.	☐	☐
8	People are provided with all the necessary resources to carry out their work.	☐	☐
9	People can access me to get any additional support or guidance should they need it.	☐	☐

Setting effective objectives

Total

Influencing people

Any performance management process clearly requires a high degree of influencing skills to achieve results. It may be easy to tell someone what they have to achieve in a classic authoritarian style, but to motivate someone to work towards a set of self-defined objectives requires a higher and more mature level of persuasive skills.

It is sometimes assumed that influencing skills, like leadership skills, are a gift that some of us are born with. This is not true as we are all capable of improving our ability and skills in influencing and persuading others. What we have to do is recognise that in order to influence others we need in the first instance to understand what motivates and drives them individually. We often get into difficulties managing other people because we wrongly assume that other people are motivated by exactly the same things as we are. Wrong! People do things for their own reasons and motivations, not ours. We also need to realise the impact that different types of influencing styles can have on people.

Many of us, because of our life and work experiences, tend to develop a relatively narrow range of influencing styles that we apply to all situations. In order to become successful influencers of people we need to be flexible in matching our influencing styles to particular situations. An understanding of the classic styles of influence can therefore be a helpful starting point.

Before using any influencing style we need to analyse the situation we are involved in, to recognise the other person's perspective and be clear about the results that we want to achieve. A little advance thought and preparation before we jump into situations can pay dividends. Indeed perhaps the most important thing to do in trying to influence others is to listen as to what the other person is actually saying.

Classic influencing styles

Key Management Concept

Influencing style/use of	Strengths	Possible pitfalls
Logic and hard analysis 'The facts of the matter are'	Ensures nothing is missed Focuses on facts and data	Can be seen as overly precise May miss emotional issues which could at the root of the issue
Criticism or Aggression 'This report is rubbish'	Involves high energy Direct and blunt Provides release for the giver	May cause an aggressive response – retaliation Often lacks precision in terms of what is said. Liable to escalate matters
Status 'I am the boss here'	Uses formal authority or executive power Easy to apply – I am the boss therefore I demand	People may either comply, become dependent, or rebel Long-term excessive use can generate sub optimal results – resentment, sabotage
Personal friendship and warmth	Develops friendly relationships and builds strong team spirit	Can, if not done well be viewed as insincere or manipulative

'Please do me a favour'	Easy to appeal to 'Can you do me a favour?' type approach	May be less appropriate where forceful decisions have to be made. If overplayed can be seen as a sign of weakness
Supportive 'We can both benefit'	Encourages individuals and building on their ideas 'Can I help or support you on that...' – helps build networks and alliances	May be seen as taking sides or having favourites
Listening and questioning to obtain views 'What are your views'	People feel their ideas are valued Leads to a full understanding	May cause anxiety if the questioning is too persistent Must be supported by a commitment or action otherwise constant questioning may cause irritation
Being open and revealing oneself 'Can I be honest with you'	Projects honesty which may facilitate full understanding Promotes high levels of trust	Can be seen by some as overly emotional and lacking in 'professionalism' May cause a 'Let's stick to the facts!' type response

Other influencing styles in detail

The following illustrate some of the most commonly employed influencing styles that we can use: when reviewing them consider your own influencing styles and reflect upon whether or not you need to consider developing other approaches. Remembering that there are no right or wrong styles. In order to be effective we need to be able to call upon a range of styles and employ them in appropriate circumstances. All too often in any influencing situation the person with the greatest range of styles and flexibility will succeed.

- **Stating your own position** – being assertive.
- **Intuitive/creative** – gut feel, hunches.
- **Logical** – the facts.
- **Supportive** – developing a common agenda.
- **Judgmental** – discriminating / criticising.
- **Clarifying the position of others** – developing an understanding.

Stating your own position – being assertive – the characteristics

- Being persistent about your needs and requirements.
- Demanding from other people.
- Declaring your needs and wants.
- Stating your rights – 'I am entitled to X'.
- Being strong without damaging others.

Statements

- I appreciate your point but I must again request the following...
- I want to make it clear to you that I expect...

- I feel you have not understood my position so let me again reiterate it...

- I need to know that you have ensured the following...

- My situation is such that I am not prepared to accept that response because...

- My concern is...

- That proposal gives me a problem because I want to...

Intuitive/creative – the characteristics

- Proposing new ideas.

- Raising alternative approaches.

- Brainstorming radical methods.

- Challenging others' methods, thinking and assumptions.

Statements

- I suggest we tackle this from a different angle.

- How about looking at the situation from another perspective.

- Here's a new idea?

- What would happen if we did...?

- Shouldn't we really be focusing on...?

- I really feel that we should be looking at some more radical alternatives...

- What if...

- Aren't we missing the point here! Surely we need to focus on x not y!...

Logical – the characteristics

- Evaluating the criteria.
- Stating the facts.
- Keeping things to the point.
- Being rational.
- Applying logic.

Statements

- Let's look at the facts.
- Simply look at the reality of the situation.
- That is simply not supported by the figures.
- The evidence does not support that approach.
- We really need to focus on the details.
- We should really keep those issues outside of the discussion.
- That is not logical.
- That idea would never work because of…
- Where is your evidence?
- How can you justify or support that argument or approach?

Supportive – the characteristics

- Involving and bringing in other people.
- Rewarding others for their contributions and efforts.
- Building on other's ideas.
- Offering positive ideas and suggestions to build on other contributions.

Statements

- I understand how you feel.

- That's an excellent idea.

- I fully appreciate your situation.

- That could prove an important issue that Max just mentioned, perhaps we should discuss it.

- I like the way you outlined the challenge.

- What if we thought about the point raised by Jean.

- I found that a helpful input on the problem.

- If we also added x to your suggestion that might also help.

Judgmental – the characteristics

- Being overly critical.

- Disagreeing.

- Highlighting obstacles.

- Seeing only problems.

Statements

- I disagree…

- That will not work because of…

- That's rubbish!

- You seem to have missed several key points.

- You have overlooked the problem of xyz.

- Yes, But…

- We seem to have a major disagreement here.
- This is getting us nowhere.
- Your analysis is overly simplistic.
- That's a preposterous idea.

Clarifying others' positions

- Drawing out other people's ideas.
- Probing for more information.
- Seeking more facts.
- Listening, showing understanding.
- Picking up unspoken feelings, non-verbal cues.

Statements

- Could you say more about that?
- What do you need to say?
- Can you give an example?
- You sound as though you have more to say about that issue?
- To sum up what you are saying...
- Could I check I have fully understood what you are saying?
- It sounds like you really feel/think that.
- I sense you are not very pleased about the issue. Is that true?
- Have I understood what you have said correctly – you are saying the following...

What influencing styles do you use?

- Do you have the right balance?

- Do you use too much of any style?

- What other styles do you need to develop to become more influential?

- Generate a list of new influencing expressions that you could practice using in meetings or other influencing situations.

Using power to influence others – where do you get yours from?

Many of us fail to realise that the authority we get in an organisation is not simply a function of our position. The fact is that there are many sources of authority that we can potentially employ to influence other people. Consider which ones you use. Ask yourself how would you manage if you lost your current sources of power tomorrow. How would you get things done?

Hierarchical	This is the power you derive based on your position in your management or organisation structure.
Information	Power that comes from having information or knowledge that others do not possess – for example your technical or market knowledge.
Expertise	Possessing a particular skill set or range of experiences that others do not.
Reputation	The power you gain from your track record and past performance. 'They always deliver the results!'
Charisma	The magic ingredient – personality, voice, appearance, energy, warmth, presence etc. Often very difficult to define but easy to identify.

Positional	This power comes from the unique nature of your role – being in a key position in a critical communication network.
Coercive	The power to punish and impose sanctions on others.

Whereas bad managers tend to rely on one or two sources of power to get things done, normally hierarchical and positional, effective managers operate from several power bases. In considering our sources of power we need to recognise that in a knowledge-based era we cannot simply rely on the power that comes to us from our position. We will need to develop other bases of power in order to influence people successfully. A greater emphasis will be placed on expertise and knowledge as key agents of influence.

To successfully succeed in influencing someone we need to analyse the situation we find ourselves in and the type of person we are dealing with. We need to reflect on the authority people possess and their aims and objectives as well as ours. We then need to be able to employ a range of influencing styles based on our interpretation of events, and avoid falling into the trap of staying with one style and so run the risk of antagonising other people. Only by being aware of all the approaches to influencing and our current preferences is it possible to identify and select the most effective style or combination to influence others. Ultimately it is all about the words we use and how we say them.

Learning to delegate effectively

Most managers complain of an excessive workload with too much to do in too little time. Learning to delegate is therefore a vital skill to master. In order to delegate effectively we need to be able to identify which of our daily tasks could be tackled by other people or members of our team. This process can then help to bring relief to a demanding and heavy workload, and also help develop other members of our team.

Before delegating any activity or task we need to consider two critical dimensions: the **importance** and **urgency** of the task.

The diagram below illustrates a simple but powerful matrix that can help us decide whether we should be holding onto a task or activity or delegating it to someone else.

Developing a personal SWOT analysis

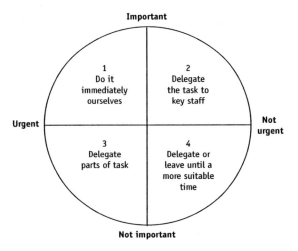

1 If a task is both urgent and important we should complete it ourselves, as quickly as possible.

2 If a task is urgent but not important it is probably most effectively tackled by some other member of the team.

3 If a task is not particularly urgent but it is important, we can either do the complete task ourselves or delegate parts of the task to team members.

4 A task that is neither important nor urgent can be left until you or someone else has time available to deal with it.

The matrix provides an easy and practical approach to thinking about our workload. Having decided that a task needs to be delegated, we then need to use our managing performance skills for managing the process. If we don't do this we may be simply 'dumping' tasks on people. We have to remember to use the Situational Leadership matrix which urged us to consider the two questions of a person's ability and motivation to do a task.

Am I delegating enough? A simple checklist

Answer these questions with a yes or no response. It will help you think about whether or not you need to be improving your skills in delegating.

		YES	NO
1	I find it difficult to delegate important tasks or work.	☐	☐
2	My team complain that they sometimes have insufficient work to do.	☐	☐
3	Team members seem to feel there is not enough challenge in their work.	☐	☐
4	I frequently believe that my team is less effective than me.	☐	☐
5	I often do tasks myself, as I find it not only quicker but that it also gives a better result.	☐	☐
6	I rarely ask myself 'Should I really be doing this?', as I know I can do it quicker and to a higher standard.	☐	☐
7	I do not allow people to make mistakes.	☐	☐
8	I explain precisely how any project or piece of work should be carried out.	☐	☐
9	I tend to work longer hours than my team.	☐	☐
10	I do not have sufficient time to train and develop my team.	☐	☐

Action Checklist

Total

Key Question

A process for managing delegation is outlined in the flow chart below:

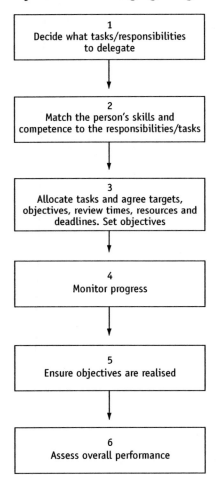

Am I the most suitable person to be doing this task?

Mastering
face-to-face
communications

No matter what your plans or strategies are as a manager, if you fail to communicate them effectively to your people you cannot expect to achieve success. Every manager or team leader needs to be an effective communicator. Communications is a skill that lies at the heart of any successful working relationship. However the main obstacle to improving our communications skills is a very simple one and it relates to our ability to listen. The fact is that most of us are bad listeners. The result is we often put our own interpretation on things that we are told and hear. This inevitably creates confusion and in some instances conflict. Problems often occur because our attention span is limited. This can happen when:

- Too much information is coming in.

- The information we are receiving is too complicated.

- We are not interested in the information.

- We disagree with what we hear.

- We disagree with what we think we hear.

- We dislike the speaker.

The result of these factors is often a failure to actively listen. In effect, we switch off! A critical skill for any manager or leader is therefore our ability to listen. To improve our communications skills we have to simply get better at listening. Effective communication is a learned behaviour and something that we can all improve.

How to really listen

Real listening involves active listening and this means demonstrating that we are interested not only in the content of what is being said but also the context of the discussion and the feelings being expressed by the other speaker. At work we are receiving information all the time – written facts, figures, presentations etc. Most of this information can be interpreted in more than one way. We all tend to interpret incoming information with reference to our past experience and what interests us, so we each have a unique perception of what is happening. Ultimately what we say and do actually depends on our interpretation and perception of the information we are receiving. A simple point to understand but quite devastating if we fail to understand its potential to corrupt our ability to communicate effectively. Quite simply put, if I decide that all accountants are incapable of communicating (because of some distant problem I had with one) I will always be negative towards any interaction I have with them. Suffice to say if we extend such leaps of illogic to other functions or areas of activity (eg Production never want to help Sales) we have a potential minefield for communications between people.

In communications remember than communications and listening involves the following:

Key Learning Point

- What is said.

- How it is said.

- What is not said.

- What is meant.

Our ability therefore to interpret information in the light of experience and select or screen out that which interests us is dangerous as much as it is invaluable in helping us become successful. On a positive note it is a vital skill that enables us to quickly make sense of what is happening, to take decisions and get things done. But it is a process that can, as we have outlined, have major disadvantages.

The fact is it is very easy for two people to have differing perceptions of the same information with the result that misunderstandings easily happen. We also need to be aware that once we have interpreted a situation in a particular way, it becomes difficult for us to see it in a different way or the full extent of the problem or opportunity.

What listening involves:

Interpretation and evaluation

This is the process that involves us 'making sense' of what we have heard. It also involves the potentially dangerous process of selective hearing whereby our existing 'mind-set' influences our reactions to the information. When we apply selective hearing we only notice selected elements of what has actually been said. In effect we listen to what we want to hear, whether it has been said or not. This is what often results in misunderstandings and conflicts with other people. We only need to think of our personal relationships to see the impact and power of this process. Parents and children often clash because of selective interpretation. 'I asked them not to come home too late and they thought I was criticising them for being irresponsible, when all I did was ask them not to come home late!'

The selective interpretation is aided by the evaluation process which involves us assessing the information we have received and deciding how to evaluate it. Even when we accurately hear what has been said and are able to make sense of it we are still subject to our own values and prejudices. Thus it is very easy to allow our feelings to influence the weighting or interpretation we give to information.

Reaction

Our reaction is therefore based on what we have heard, our interpretation and final evaluation of the information. Whatever our reactions we all give some feedback that indicates whether we have understood what has been said. This reaction is not only conveyed in what we might say but also in our voice and intonation.

Six fundamental questions you can ask yourself about your communications style

What am I trying to say?

Make sure you clearly understand the information or message you are trying to convey. When communicating be precise and succinct. Remember that fewer words are often better than too many.

What do I want to achieve?

Make sure the words you choose to communicate are really going to support you in achieving your goals. Do you need to support your verbal communication with any visual material? Be clear about what you want to achieve – a reaction, agreement, or a decision?

Am I sticking to the facts?

Make sure the information you are providing is accurate and not influenced by opinion unless a personal element is essential to your objective . In cases where you want people to act they can only make a decision or act appropriately when they have all the facts. Check whether you are providing all the necessary information available to help the other person understand.

Can I deliver on my commitments?

In certain situations it is often tempting to promise something to win people over, especially when faced with a difficult situation and time pressures. But remember that a subsequent failure to deliver on promises generates disappointment and ultimately erodes trust – and trust is one of the fundamentals of good communication. So if you are providing any commitments remember to be prepared to deliver.

Am I prepared to follow up?

Effective communications between a manager and their people must be an ongoing process and not a one-off activity. Always be prepared to answer follow up questions and queries; accepting feedback as part of your normal commitment to being seen as an effective communicator.

Am I credible?

If you are new to a management position then a degree of distance from your people can inevitably follow. So you may need to make a deliberate effort take an interest in your people. Be available to them – and above all, be honest in your dealings with them. If you follow these guidelines you will develop trust and in turn good communications with your people will follow.

So remember that effective communications is about what people say to you as much as what you say to them. It is also vital to remember that people do have a tremendous capacity to receive your messages in different ways. We are all influenced by personalities, values, and relationships.

So take time to check out that people have understood what you have said. With smaller, open corporate structures and fewer layers of managers, effective communication is more important than ever: it is vital that we get it right.

Action Checklist

Communications checklist

When communicating do:

- Make eye contact with the other person – it demonstrates trust, honesty and shows interest. Try to identify the colour of their eyes at a first contact or handshake.

- Check your understanding of what has been said to you by summarising, paraphrasing or reflecting back to the speaker.

- Make sure your body language and tone of voice reflect interest – try leaning towards the speaker, and respond with a questioning or reflective tone of voice.

- Convey enthusiasm in your voice.

- Listen for feelings as well as facts. Too often we listen only for facts – which may account for only 20% of the issue or problem.

When communicating don't:

- Interrupt the other person as they talk.

- Finish off the end of their sentences.

- Let your mind wander during the discussion.

- Spend listening time thinking about your next question.

- Focus on one small aspect of the discussion and miss the main part of the message.

Remember the facts about communications

- About 80% of our waking hours are spent communicating. We spend 45% of this time listening.

- In meetings we spend about 60-70 % of our time listening.

- After a ten minute presentation we only hear, understand, evaluate and retain approximately 50% of what is said. After 48 hours this can fall to as little as 25%.

- Remember our listening habits are not the result of training but rather the lack of it.

Listening and communicating to others – some basic rules

There are a number of effective communications processes that we can practice without too much difficulty. These processes can help us overcome the obstacles caused by different perceptions and listening difficulties. They help us to stay 'on the same wavelength' as the person we are dealing with and so become more effective when communicating .

- **Stop talking** – you can't listen while you are talking. It is very easy to get carried away by our own thoughts. So try to pause at frequent intervals to give the other person a chance to react. Some people never invite a response from the person they are talking to and then express surprise that they switch people off.

- **Give your listener an overview or summary of what you want to say** before launching into detail. This allows the other person the chance to put into context what you are trying to say.

- **Empathise** with the other person – when someone is trying to explain something try to put yourself in their position so that you can understand and see what they are trying to communicate. The ability to empathise is very important when dealing with difficult or emotional situations.

- **If you want to speak, signal for attention**, eg raise the palm of your hand and say 'Can I comment on that?' and pause before commenting. This gives the other person the opportunity to pause and switch their attention to you before you speak.

- **Ask questions** – when you don't understand something that is being said or when you need clarification of a point. This clearly indicates that you are listening. However avoid asking questions that embarrass people or highlight their lack of knowledge unless it is absolutely necessary.

Tactics such as these often cause hostility resentment leading to a breakdown of communications.

- **Don't stop listening too quickly** – don't interrupt people – give them time to finish speaking.

- **Concentrate on what the person is really saying, not what you think they are saying** – actively focus your attention on their words, ideas and feelings.

- **Look at the other person** – watch their face, mouth, eyes, and body language. Observing someone's body language will help you understand how they feel about what they are saying. Mirror or reflect back their body language in a sensitive manner as this will help you to show that you are listening and trying to develop a rapport.

- **Summarise what the other person has said at key intervals** – this helps you to clarify your understanding and to clear up any misunderstandings.

- **Leave any emotional baggage behind** – if you can, try to push your emotions, fears or problems outside the meeting room. Factors such as these can often prevent you from listening. But at other times recognise that you may well need to discuss people's feelings in order to get to the real issues.

- **Control your anger** – try not to get angry at what is being said. Whilst anger can be a positive force it can often prevent you from actively listening and developing a true understanding of what is being said. If you do feel strongly about an issue, recognise your feelings but then try to isolate and control them for the discussion.

- **Remove distractions** – put down any papers or pencils you have in your hands as they can cause distractions when communicating.

- **Focus on the critical points** – concentrate on the important ideas and not the detailed points. Of course detail is important, but it is often not as important as the critical points being made in a discussion. Getting agreement or understanding of the big issues is often the breakthrough in discussions. So examine the detail but only to subsequently prove, support or define the main thrust of what is being said or agreed.

- **If you disagree with what is being said**, don't begin by stating that you disagree. This approach often provokes an unreceptive response from the other person. Instead explain your position first and then add why you find it necessary to disagree.

- **Share responsibility for effective communications** – only part of the responsibility for communication lies with the person speaking; as a listener you have an equally important role. Work hard at understanding what is being said and if you don't, ask for clarification.

- **Evaluate the facts and evidence** – as you listen, try to identify not only the significance of the facts and evidence but also their relevance to the discussion.

- **React to ideas, not to people** – don't allow your reactions to the person speaking to influence your interpretation of what they are saying. Remember someone else's ideas or opinions may be valid even if you don't personally like the person or the way they look.

- **Use the speaking and listening differential** – we can all listen faster than we can talk. By using this differential to our advantage we can really stay focused and concentrate on what has been said. Our speech rate is 100 to 150 words per minute; our ability to listen and think is up to 250 to 500 words per minute.

- **Listen for what is not said** – sometimes you can learn just as much by determining what the other person has not said as by what they have said. But in doing this you need to be aware of the dangers of selective interpretation, so you need to listen incredibly hard not just for the facts but also the feelings and if possible the underlying values being expressed.

- **Listen to how something is said** – we frequently concentrate so hard on what is said that we miss the importance of the emotional reactions and attitudes being voiced in someone's speech. In certain cases the attitudes and emotions surrounding a situation may be more important than the words being spoken.

- **Don't antagonise the other person** – we can sometimes cause someone else to conceal their ideas, emotions or attitudes by antagonising them. This might be achieved by arguing, criticising or not asking questions. So try to be aware of the effect you are having on the other person.

- **Listen for the real person** – one of the best ways of finding out about a person is to listen to them talk. By listening to someone talk you can begin to discover what they like and dislike, what their motivations are, what their values are and what makes them tick.

- **Avoid jumping to assumptions** – the old adage states that assumptions can make an ASS out of U and ME. Assumptions can be extremely dangerous so don't assume other people use words the same way you do, 'they didn't say what they meant, but you understand what they meant'. Don't assume that that they are avoiding looking you in the eye because they are telling a lie; that they are trying to embarrass you by looking you in the eye; that they are lying because they have interpreted the facts differently than you have, or that they are angry because they are enthusiastic in presenting their views. Assumptions like these may turn out to be true, but more often they just get in the way of clear understanding.

- **Avoid stereotyping the other person** – too often we try to box a person to fit everything they say into what makes sense to us. They are a 'compromiser' or 'difficult person'. Therefore, our perceptions of what they say or mean are all shaded by whether we like or dislike people who compromise. At times, it helps in understanding people to know their values and motivations, but we all have the capacity to be unpredictable and to not fit into convenient stereotypes.

- **Avoid quick judgements** – wait until you have established all the facts before making any judgements on a person or situation.

- **Recognise your own prejudices** – try to be aware of your own feelings towards other people and allow for these prejudices.

- **Identify the influencing style being used** – listen for the influencing style being used by the speaker: logic, emotion, authority.

Applying classic questioning techniques

Your ability to ask questions is another critical skill in developing a high level of inter-personal communications. We all need to be able to employ a wide range of different questions in order that we can use them to:

- Gather information on issues.

- Explore people's feelings and attitudes.

- Provoke thought and further discussion.

- Help someone think through a problem.

- Seek clarification on a point or issue.

- See how somebody reacts or responds (style, method etc).

As we have already emphasised, as managers we are sometimes better at talking than asking questions, so developing a toolkit of effective questions can be a valuable asset. Listed below are the classic types of questions we use:

- Open-ended
- Closed
- Extending
- Leading
- Loaded
- Multiple

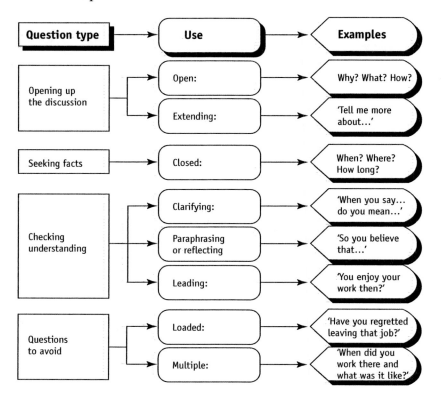

Key Learning Point

Action point

How to effectively answer questions with confidence

- Thank the person for their question and pause for a moment to reflect and gather your thoughts.

- Repeat the question to confirm that you have understood it correctly.

- Answer the question as best as you can – being direct and succinct.

- Check with the person that you have answered the question to their satisfaction – remember this is not the same as having given them the answer they wanted!

- Thank the individual for their question and interest.

Auditing your listening – key skills

Below is quick guide to identifying if you are a good or bad listener. To improve your skills try to apply the rules and avoid the bad behaviours, or at least be conscious of them.

Key listening rules	The bad listener	The good listener
Try to identify areas of common interest or ground	Rejects boring subjects	Asks 'What's in it for me?'
Assess the content of what is said and not just the delivery	Rejects message and information if the delivery is poor or distracting	Listens for content. Able to overcome errors and mannerisms
Don't evaluate too quickly what is said	Argues	Clarifies before commenting
Listen for any ideas that may lie behind what is being said	Listens only for facts, concepts or feelings	Listens for issues, themes
Avoid external distractions	Is easily distracted	Fights or avoids distractions, tolerates bad habits and knows how to concentrate
Exercise your brain when faced with something new or difficult	Rejects/refuses difficult materials	Views complex material as a challenge/opportunity to learn
Try to stay open-minded	Rejects emotional words or issues	Interprets emotionally charged words or statements. Does not ignore them

Understanding the impact of non-verbal communications

We cannot __not__ communicate – the way we move and use our physiology sends lots of messages and we need to recognise this fact.

The non-verbal signs or body language that we give when communicating to other people can have a powerful impact on any communications process. In order to understand the non-verbal messages we send we need to consider the following signals:

Eye contact

Typically, when people are talking they do not look at the listener all the time. Rather, they will focus around the individual to gauge reaction, then give a longer look to signal that they expect some verbal response. Eye contact by the listener suggests interest. A steady gaze is often associated with trust and confidence. However, in some situations a sustained gaze could be interpreted as a stare and possibly even aggressive, if other non-verbal behaviours do not give a more sympathetic impression.

Physical proximity

This of course varies in different cultures. So for some people 'keeping your distance' may appear naturally polite, for others, a sign of remoteness and even hostility. The safest guideline is to try to establish a comfortable distance, but bear in mind that if you keep backing away to preserve your 'personal space', your actions may be misinterpreted.

Body posture

The body posture that we adopt can convey a lot of information about how we feel or think about a situation. Crossed arms, for instance, are often viewed as a sign of defensiveness – at the same time they can simply mean that the person is comfortable. Conversely open arms are likely to suggest interest and concern. Leaning forward can demonstrate interest, although when overdone it may be seen as threatening. Leaning back can show either disinterest, or being relaxed depending on other cues such as the level of questions being asked.

Leaning forward too much can suggest aggression, whereas leaning forward gently indicates interest in what is being said and can do much to build rapport.

Key Learning Point

Action point

How you use your physiology – the way you move, speak and project energy is a major component of influencing other people. Skilled influencers often project strong levels of physical energy. When they move they use their body language in a positive manner. They don't slouch or appear slow.

- They offer a strong and firm handshake.
- They speak with an effective voice tone and vary the pace to emphasise key points.
- They move swiftly and with energy.
- They gesticulate and use strong hand movements – forcefully tapping a table, using a pointing figure to people or downwards towards a table.
- They using sweeping hand movements to involve people.
- They will invade other people's space – moving in on them to impose themselves.
- They stand up in meetings and walk around.

So think about your body language and how you project your physiology to other people. Can you do more to project influence?

Physical gestures

Physical gestures can vary a lot between cultures and is therefore a potential minefield. But there are some classic behaviours we can all look out for. For example a nodding head is usually taken in most Anglo Saxon cultures as a sign of agreement or understanding. In addition by nodding you will usually encourage someone else to continue talking. In contrast the classic 'looking at your watch' can signal boredom or a need to move on and, when used, provided the person is sensitive to these things will usually bring proceedings to a swift conclusion.

Also watch for classic symptoms such as:

- Folded arms (disinterest, bored – although in some cultures this denotes attention and respect).

- Leaning back in a chair (relaxed and comfortable).

- Head in hands (Boredom, disinterest).

- No eye contact (Bored, shy, lacking confidence, distrust – just from this simple list you see the potential dangers of misinterpreting such behaviours).

Hands

When someone's hands are not used in conjunction with someone's speech this can indicate a nervousness and a need to develop further rapport. Conversely we will all be familiar with hand wringing or clenched knuckles as indicating anxiety or mounting tension.

The movement of hands to the face or mouth can also indicate some form of discomfort or stress. Possibly touching an ear lobe indicates a negative evaluation with what has been said or a refusal to accept the information. Some people argue that a hand to mouth when they are speaking suggests that a lie or untruth is being spoken. Others argue that putting fingers to the mouth indicates a desire to interrupt the other speaker.

Stroking the chin is believed to indicate thought and a weighing up of what is being said. Whereas when an index finger is pointed vertically towards a lip and the other fingers rest underneath the chin suggests that a critical evaluation is taking place.

Facial expressions

These are perhaps more obvious than other cues, since we all know how to 'look bored' and show 'delight'. So as well as trying to spot others' behaviours try to remain aware of your own facial expressions and use them to your advantage. The effective deployment of facial expressions can be critical in negotiating or sales type meetings. If you sense problems with another person as a result of their expressions check them out. 'You look surprised, shocked by that comment?'

Voice tone and other verbal cues

'That's very interesting' spoken in a monotone voice is unlikely to convince anyone that you are interested in what they are saying. So don't betray any personal feelings or opinions though your voice tone as it is an easy give away to other people.

'Mm', 'aha' every now and again will help to keep your speaker talking. Avoid 'err' or 'ugh' as they can sometimes suggest a lack of confidence, or lack of attention.

Mastering role reviews and coaching techniques

Chapter 5

Appraising your people

An overview

Appraising someone's performance is a critical management activity. It can lead to promotions, salary increases, transfers or in some cases dismissal. All appraisal schemes are based on the assumption that people like to know how they are doing in their work. However, appraisal interviews have not always been popular with managers because some dislike having to give someone bad news about their performance. Many appraisal schemes use such traits as insight and creativity which, though important, are difficult to assess objectively. Experience shows that although managers prefer conducting appraisal interviews with objective data they are not always happy with the concept of face to face judgement of staff. Perhaps one of the reasons for this is that we sometimes know that our people are likely to be more aware than us as to whether a performance standard has been met in 'spirit as well as the letter'. As a result some managers can distrust this lack of precision and believe the appraisal process is too subjective. People who are on the end of the process can also sometimes share this view.

But despite these concerns the real benefits of any effective 'Performance Management' or appraisal process is that it can be based on agreed objectives. At the same time it enables a structured discussion to be carried out between a manager and team member.

In talking about performance appraisals we prefer to use the term **role review** as it more adequately reflects the change away from jobs, which have connotations of rigid territorial ownership. Roles differ to jobs in the sense that they are more fluid and dynamic and more suited to current and future organisational needs for flexibility.

The objectives of role reviews

If any role review is to be of value it must have as its main focus people's current and future work challenges and problems. Thus the interview must result in the following:

- The identification of current and future work challenges, problems and priorities.

- Agreement on plans for resolving issues in the above areas.

- The identification of any learning, development or training needs.

- Planned and agreed actions to meet training and learning needs.

A successful role review must focus on the future and only draw on past experiences, achievements or failures as a way of clarifying future actions. Success in any role review depends on the extent to which an atmosphere of openness, trust and mutual respect can be established.

In looking at the details involved in running an effective role review we need to examine the basic benefits that result from the process for the individual, manager and organisation.

The individual

Everybody likes and needs to know how they are performing in their work. We also enjoy having an opportunity to discuss our work in detail and to explore or find out how we might improve and develop our abilities and potential.

The manager

As managers an effective review will help us to achieve a detailed understanding of our people's views on their performance and work. We will also benefit from a discussion on their future aspirations and be able to identify any additional help or resources they might need or are seeking from other parts of the organisation.

The process helps us understand or discover any individual areas of confusion or overlap in our team's roles. It provides an opportunity to review performance in detail as opposed to the casual five minute 'snapshot' discussions that characterise many of our day to day management activities.

The organisation

For the organisation a role review can help generate stronger working relationships and link individual efforts to overall corporate performance. It also highlights and focuses people on corporate priorities and identifies people with potential as well as contributing to the identification of training and learning needs.

Guide to Best Practice

Structuring a role review

Role reviews should be held on a regular basis, at least three to four times a year. The purpose being to review the contribution of the individual in terms of their:

- Progress in achieving objectives.

- Need to modify objectives either by increasing the standards of performance, or adjusting them to take account of any adverse influences that may be impacting on their performance.

- Agreement to priority and non-priority objectives included in the next set of improvement plans.

In conducting any role review it is also critical to ensure that the:

- Forward planning element is the most important.

- Focus on past performance plays a secondary part.

- Review provides an opportunity and environment for the manager and individual to exchange views.

- Manager provides coaching and guidance.

Too many managers think that a role review can be conducted without too much preparation and conducted 'on the run'. This invariably proves incorrect and leads to surprises for both the manger and role holder. Preparation is key to getting the right result. You must know the facts and establish what the performance issues are. Too many role reviews fail because managers do not do their homework properly.

You also need to remember that a role interview, perhaps more than another time during the year, puts you as a manager under review. Your staff will be looking to see if you have considered it an important enough event to take out quality time to prepare. So you need to recognise that a lack of preparation on your part may be rightly interpreted by your staff as disinterest in them.

A typical structure for a role review meeting

Meeting Phase	Initiative taken by Role Holder	Manager	Principal Activity	Balance of Time Spent on Activity
Past Performance Review	50%	50%	1 Review overall progress in a 3 or 6 month period 2 Review key tasks and achievements 3 Check results against targets 4 Consider performance and future challenges	25-35%
Future Targets and Development Plans	75%	75%	5 Identify current issues, obstacles, challenges to future performance 6 Develop new agreed performance plans and targets from previous results 7 Identify any other issues of concern 8 Identify development and learning needs 9 Personal coaching and guidance provided by manager	65-75%

The need for preparation

The following problems can arise at role reviews, particularly in the early stages of a meeting:

- An over-emphasis on reviewing the documentation of objectives.

- Too strong a focus on looking back (up to 80/90% of discussion time) thus leaving little or no time for looking ahead to future performance.

- Being too rigid with the interview structure. A role review needs to be a fluid and dynamic process resulting in a genuine exploration of issues and problems.

- Individuals becoming defensive in the face of a manager taking too critical or directive a role.

- Failure to be clear as to what your people have been doing – in other words not doing your homework.

These problems can be overcome by:

- Careful preparation for the review by both the role holder and manager.

- Encouraging role holders to take the initiative in the discussion. Ask them to comment on their performance, successes and disappointments.

This last point does not mean that as a manager you lose control of the review. It is your role to judge progress and manage the meeting to ensure that all critical items are discussed.

There may be a role review where it seems that there are so many problems to be discussed, that even 3 or 4 hours would not be long enough. In such extreme cases it is advisable to restrict the meeting to say 2 hours and make arrangements for another separate meeting.

Key Learning Point

Action points

The key elements of successful role reviews

- There needs to be a formal structure to the review meeting.

- The role holder needs to feel at ease, and be encouraged to participate and take the initiative.

- Interruptions should be avoided at all costs.

- The room should be comfortable and reflect the right atmosphere – not next to the production department.

- The discussion needs to have a future orientation rather than an inquest or post-mortem on the past.

- The meeting needs to be seen as an integral part of the organisation's normal process for managing people and performance.

Guide to Best Practice

Getting ready for a role review interview

Preparing for the interview

Prior to any review you should have agreed a time with your team member and asked them to think through their role, current performance and work problems and identify where they think they need help. In your role as a coach you should prepare by reviewing:

- Records of performance.

- Projects they have been involved with.

- Future workloads and problems.

- Possible development opportunities.

- The environment and arrangements for the interview.

At this stage of the process you should refrain from pre-judging the performance even though this will be difficult. Save any thoughts or opinions you may have until you have got the views of your team member at the interview.

Creating the right atmosphere for the review

As an effective coach you need to create an open and frank atmosphere during the review. So ensure that:

- **You gain initial agreement with the individual about the review's purpose.** Establish some ground rules about openness and frankness. Unless you have this established the right climate your review is a non-starter and your team member will feel under suspicion or examination: neither of which are conducive to having a fundamental discussion about performance.

- **You have set aside ample time for the review.** 'This meeting is important and two hours has been set aside for it to ensure that we can have a quality discussion without interruption.' You might use this as an introductory opening to emphasise your commitment.

- **Your team member has ample opportunity during the meeting to voice their views and opinions.** You should encourage them to state their thoughts and clarify any problems or issues with you.

- **You focus on successes as well as problem areas** – successes can more easily be built upon than failures.

- **You challenge on issues you appear to disagree over.** Where necessary you may need to be direct and explain why you disagree. Use examples to illustrate your points. Remember failure to challenge positively and in a timely way may result in problems being allowed to develop later on. So be assertive and direct when discussing matters that concern you.

- **You gain commitment.** Avoid friendly discussions which fail to clarify who is responsible for any problems or agreed actions. Set the time scales and agree who is responsible for what.

As an effective coach you may need to be prepared to change your opinion during the course of a review. Demonstrating a high degree of flexibility in outlook and approach will go a long way to stimulating a positive and constructive dialogue.

If you need to criticise, you should do so constructively, explaining why certain decisions or actions were wrong in your view. Then discuss them to check that the individual has understood your point of view. Always providing positive alternative actions or suggestions to help the person cope with the same situation the next time. Simply criticising poor performance might provide you with some short term relief but it does little to help the receiver overcome the problem the next time. It is part of your job as a coach to help redirect the person by offering positive alternative strategies.

Also remember that development is another prime aim of any role review. The process must not be seen as relating solely to salary, promotion, discipline. It is essential that you ensure this is made clear from the outset of the review. Setting aside time to discuss learning and development needs are key.

Dealing with reactions during a role review

Insufficient skill on your part, or your team member, may result in difficult reactions during a review. The way in which you deal with such reactions can either destroy the review or put it back on track. We have listed below some potential reactions that you might experience when carrying out reviews. There are also suggested responses for dealing with them:

- **Your team member accepts your assessment and is willing to improve.** The majority of people will react in this way provided your review has been objective and constructive. Even so, do not underestimate the need for positive feedback and praise. At the same time you should have prepared some new opportunities and challenges to discuss.

- **Your team member disagrees with your views and supplies facts to support their case.** In this situation total agreement may be impossible to achieve during the review. Areas of agreement should be confirmed and areas of disagreement should be freely discussed. At the end of the session you may need to say 'We'll leave that aside and I'll check on the facts and we can meet again'. But if the person is right you may have to simply accept that you got it wrong and agree with them. If you have agreed to go away and check you must ensure that you follow things up. Otherwise you will lose credibility.

- **Your team member accepts criticism too easily; adopting a passive role and accepting criticism without responding.** This can be a real problem in the sense that you may feel the individual is not taking the review seriously. To counter this you might ask the individual to summarise your criticisms and to comment on them further. In such cases you might wish to provoke some kind of reaction from them. So try a slightly provocative statement such as 'You don't seem very interested or bothered by all of this' or 'What do you think will happen if this situation continues?' This might generate a reaction.

- **Your team member denies the points you are making and passes the buck.** Buck passing whereby someone else is blamed for problems is a common flaw with people who are faced with receiving negative feedback. Of course in some circumstances it may be fully justified. If you do not feel the individual is justified in arguing such a case, you should together analyse one or more of the specific circumstances in depth. You need to explore the situation fully and get to the fundamental points.

- **Your team member reacts emotionally.** If someone gets angry or cries because of having to hear negative criticism don't argue back with them or disapprove of any emotional outburst. Simply remain calm and absorb their outburst by listening. If the individual really is too emotionally upset to continue, stop the interview and resume it at a later date. Alternatively, let the emotions subside naturally and continue the review.

Remember, in some cases people will break down to avoid confronting difficult news. In effect they may be trying to manipulate you to give up the session by appealing to your emotions. In such situations be careful as invariably you will have to deal with the issue another day. So if you expect tears be prepared in advance – give the person the chance to compose themselves and continue in a calm and rational manner. If necessary offer them a cup of tea but make sure you continue in a calm and composed manner.

- **Your team member is passive and unresponsive.** This response may require you to remove any fears or misunderstandings that may be present by further explaining what the review is all about. If this does not create a positive response you should concentrate on anything in which the individual shows an interest, even if to start with it is not related to the purpose of the review. You need to find out why they are reacting as they are. Are they bored, fed up or annoyed about something?

Key Learning Point

Remember to close any role review on a positive note. Summarise what has been agreed by whom and by when. Thank them for their time and input. Wish them well for the future.

A quick guide to running successful role reviews

Have a positive attitude

- Be clear that the review is for the benefit of the individual, yourself, and your organisation.

- Expect the results of the review to have a positive impact.

- Look at the review as an essential part of your role as a professional manager.

Be prepared

- Spend time and effort preparing for each review. Think of the effort you would like your manager to put into the process.

- When analysing the individual's performance list major strengths and weaknesses, then identify specific examples of each. Provide specific suggestions for future action.

- Use a performance review form as a working tool to document points and agreed actions.

- Arrange a time for the review and provide a copy of the performance review form so your team member can also be prepared and be ready to compare performance notes.

Conduct an open review

- Be honest, objective, and constructive.

- Promote a genuine discussion Allow people to present their ideas and listen to them. Be willing to change your position if your facts are proved wrong.

- Keep comments specific. Relate them to the performance and goals set during the last review session and to the individual's performance. Comments should be consistent with the feedback received during their normal day to day work. Springing surprises on unsuspecting people creates only bigger problems!

- Avoid statements based on personality unless they really do impact on job performance. If they do, be descriptive. Describe the effect on job performance, not the personality problem. For example, 'The way you speak to customers is too aggressive, for example last week you said to…'. This type of specific feedback is much more constructive than saying you have a bad attitude, as it forces the individual to respond to your specific observations.

- Avoid the tendency to omit negative comments for fear of being disliked. The purpose of the review is to help the individual: by avoiding the unpleasant, you only hurt the individual and yourself. Don't run from the unpleasant elements. If you don't you will almost invariably have to face them at another time and the chances are that by then they will be bigger problems.

- Remember that we all have weaknesses and strengths. Discuss both with your people.

Reach an agreement

- Be sure the other person understands and accepts the review. Let them summarise what was discussed and agreed to be sure that there are no misunderstandings.

- Together you should arrive at a consensus of past performance and a realistic action plan for the future. This plan should include ways to capitalise on their strengths and deal with any problem areas or development needs.

- Both of you should contract to confirm in writing your discussion and any agreements.

Don't forget about it

- Completion of the review itself does not conclude your obligation. Make sure you provide ongoing support and guidance to the person involved.

- Follow up later with the individual to ensure that agreed action plans were accomplished.

Mastering poor performers

Chapter 6

How to deal with poor performers

Sooner or later all managers, no matter how effective they are, have to deal with a difficult person or poor performer. It is always easy to give good news to someone but for most of us the prospect of having to give bad news presents a more challenging task. Many managers feel deeply uncomfortable about having to give negative feedback for fear of provoking a hostile reaction, damaging relationships or simply upsetting someone. But the fact is that managing sometimes involves telling people things that they may not want to hear.

Giving negative feedback constructively severely tests a manager's people skills, so it is crucial to know not just how to do it but also how to deal with the problems that can arise. Dealing with poor performers requires us to draw on certain areas of knowledge that we have already referred to, such as objective setting and influencing skills.

Some classic problem people types that we may have to deal with may include the:

- **Excuse giver** I couldn't because of ......

- **Fault finder** But it was the logistics' department fault.

- **Whinger** But the equipment was not up to scratch.

- **Late deliverer** It will be ready in another week, I promise.

- **Inept** Sorry I didn't realise.

- **Slow learner** I just need a bit more time to get the hang of things.

Each of these characters must be dealt with in a structured and formal manner if they are to made to realise the error of their ways.

Managing poor performers – a quick route map

Guide to Best Practice

*Managing the
performance gap*

Establish the existing performance gap	• Check the facts on performance. • Check the objectives you previously agreed. • Always focus on the facts and issues not the personality.
Explore the performance gap	• Use open questions (what, when, where, how and who).
Ask	• Why is it happening? What factors are creating the gap?

Listen to the answers being given	• Find out whether the problem is due to:
	  – personal grievances
	  – personal problems (ill health, home difficulties etc)
	  – outdated rules/procedures
	  – genuine discipline problem
	  – personality(s) clashes
	  – unclear objectives
	  – need for more training or help on the job.
	  – incompetence.

Eliminate the performance gap	• Agree an improvement plan if it is clear that poor performance is not the result of a grievance or personal problem.

Agreeing performance targets

After having discussed the performance problems the next step is to agree some new performance targets and ensure that you set some clear objectives. Use the SMART acronym to focus the problem person and begin to effect an improvement in their performance.

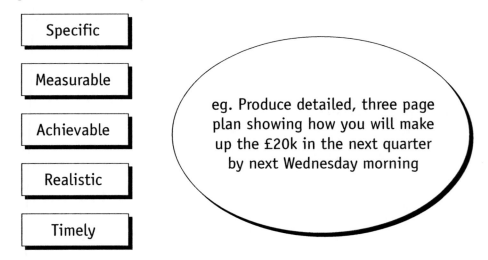

Specific

Measurable

Achievable

Realistic

Timely

eg. Produce detailed, three page plan showing how you will make up the £20k in the next quarter by next Wednesday morning

Agree a specific date to agree when you will both meet to review progress.

If it is a grievance or personal problem which is causing the poor performance:

1   Resolve the problem on the spot: re-allocate work, explain and deal with whatever is worrying the person or whatever else may be the formula to redress the grievance.

OR

2   Promise to go away and think the point over. State that you will come back to them with an answer within X amount of time.

The poor performance caricatures

The type	Their behaviour
Roger The Dodger	'Didn't you get my message'
The Injured Bystander	'Surely you are not accusing me'
The Confessor	'Yes, I know it's all my fault...'
The Buck Passer	'Yes, if only sales had not taken so long...'
The Part Time Lawyer	'All of us think...'
The Fox	Hardly speaks – except to seek further explanation.
The Cry baby	Uses tears and emotion to weaken management's resolve.
The Resigner	'Well, if that's the way you feel I guess I will have to re-consider my position.'
The Depressive	'I know I'm useless...'
The Counter Attacker	'Are you telling me how to do my job?'

With each of these people the solution is to:-

• Be firm.

• Stick to the facts and get them to address the real issues.

• Get them to explain specific behaviours or actions rather than generalities.

- Pin them down to **agree to** and **deliver** specific changes within certain times.

- Then monitor their performance.

How to give negative feedback successfully

Giving feedback is the way we either recognise successes or deliver negative news about someone's professional or technical competence or their interpersonal communications.

Feedback can of course be based on clear performance standards or opinions. When using the latter, we must ensure any feedback we give is fair and based on some kind of real evidence or facts. Failure to do so may result in conflicts or disputes arising.

Giving feedback normally involves us conveying:

Empathy

By displaying active listening and demonstrating understanding. Avoiding and resisting any immediate judgements or reactions.

Respect

Through sharing feelings and respecting people's rights and sense of integrity and self respect.

Genuineness

By reflecting and talking about experiences that maybe appropriate to the circumstances. Being sincere and adopting a positive and constructive tone throughout the discussion.

Using the praise sandwich technique: a quick checklist

As we have said, whilst it is easy to praise an individual it is often more difficult to give bad news or feedback on poor performance. The following rules relate to what is commonly called the praise sandwich. Before using this technique it is important to recognise that you have to be in the business of developing long–term capability. If you are two weeks short of dismissing someone then the approach outlined below will not be appropriate. This approach demands a desire to engage in a long–term working relationship which is based on developing someone's capability and potential:

- **Start with a positive comment** – if a positive is registered first, any subsequent negative is more likely to be listened to and acted upon.

- **Be specific and focus only on the individual's behaviour** – pinpoint behaviour that people are able to change – ' In chairing meetings you tend to talk over people'. Follow this feedback with specific examples 'for example last Monday...'.

- **Describe the event** – ' You give vague instructions'. Don't evaluate by giving more emotive feedback such as 'You give terrible instructions'. This always inflames feelings.

- **Use 'I' statements** –' I feel that you...'. This makes the feedback more concrete and more likely to be listened to – after all it is your view that you are expressing, not a universal truth!

- **Ask whether the other person can see your point of view** – and whether they can think of anything they can do differently.

- **Suggest alternative ways of approaching the problem** – give them a clue about the outcome you would prefer.

- **Don't overload** – people can only handle up to three pieces of negative feedback in one session.

Receiving feedback

As the receiver of feedback, you may be selective in what you hear. To avoid this common problem you may like to observe the following rules:

- Listen first, postpone any initial reactions.

- Be clear about what's being said.

- Probe until there is something you can act on.

- Check with others to verify the validity of the comments.

- Remember it is your choice whether to accept or reject the feedback.

Action point avoiding the Piggy Bank Syndrome

A trap that many managers fall into when managing their people is to avoid giving negative feedback at an early and appropriate stage. All too often we fail to deliver the negative feedback at the time when the problem incident occurred. Instead we collect the problems in a mental piggy back until such time that the individual makes such a mistake or problem that we then break open our piggy bank and confront the individual with a tirade of past misdemeanours. Unfortunately this all to often results in a reaction from the individual 'But you never told me that' or 'I didn't know that'!

The ten rules of feedback

All these rules spring from the fundamental principle that people have a right to their individuality and integrity.

1 Offer feedback on people behaviour(s), not their attitudes.

What you saw someone actually doing, rather than what you think they were thinking or intending; 'You were gripping that pencil so tightly that your knuckles went white' rather than 'You were very aggressive'.

2 Offer a description of what you saw and how you felt, rather than a judgement.

'When you started to shout, I felt anxious' rather than 'It was a bad idea to raise your voice'.

3 Focus on behaviour(s) which can be changed.

It is not helpful to tell someone that an eye twitch is a distraction. A persistent drumming on the table with a hand or tapping of the foot, can however be changed and so you can give feedback on these points.

4 Select behaviours or issues that are critical – limit yourself to those.

Nobody can concentrate on changing everything at once. Set priorities before you give feedback and concentrate on important points, not minor details.

5 Ask questions of the other person rather than make statements.

By asking questions we allow the person receiving the feedback the responsibility to reach their own conclusions about the issues.
'What do you think will happen if this situation continues?'
rather than
'You need to pull your socks up and get sorted out!'

6 Establish the ground rules in advance.

Tell people by what criteria or standards they are to be judged by.

7 Comment on the positives, as well as the problems – but be sincere!

It is important that people feel strengthened by any feedback process if they are to work on improving their performance. If feedback leaves them feeling inadequate or humiliated, it will have been counter-productive.

At the same time It is particularly important to realise that any praise is sincere. People see through comments that lack sincerity.

8 Relate feedback to specific behaviours: don't waffle on about general feelings or impressions.

'I liked it when you went to the door to let him in' is preferable to 'There was a very friendly atmosphere'. Because the feedback is specific the person receiving it can learn from it and replicate the behaviour again. You cannot 'do' a friendly atmosphere again.

9 Observe personal limits.

If you overload people with negative feedback they may turn off or in some cases become hostile. Recognise that we all have tolerance levels that should not be breached.

10 Before offering feedback consider its value for the receiver.

If there is no benefit to be given keep quiet and forget about it.

Finally, remember to keep any negative feedback you give private and confidential – preserve people's integrity and self respect.

Mastering team management

Chapter 7

An introduction to team performance

As managers we all spend considerable amounts of time managing our teams. But despite this investment many of us continue to be critical of our teams and the way they work. Typical comments we might hear include:

'They just don't work for each other.'

'The team review meeting is just another opportunity for them to moan about their needs.'

'Our best ideas seem to get lost in team meetings.'

'They just don't seem interested or motivated.'

'Absolutely chaotic!! Everyone was all over the place!'

Clearly these sorts of comments indicate underlying problems with team performance.

In our rapidly changing world of organisations words such as empowerment have been joined by an increased emphasis on teams and the concept of team based working. As organisational structures are in a state of constant flux so project working has become a key feature of working. Teams are now felt to assume greater importance and significance. Managers are expected to establish teams more rapidly and to motivate them to high levels of performance. The way today's organisations work involve constantly creating and breaking up teams. This is a trend that looks set to continue and so we need to get smarter at understanding the dynamics of high performance teams in order to build effective teams and get behind any problems.

So what is a team? Well a team maybe defined as a unified group of people who have their own areas of responsibility within the team, but who need the resources and support of other team members to accomplish objectives.

Work teams may be called task forces, project groups, committees or work groups. In some respects they might be identified with football teams. To score a goal, the team must play together. Just as a football team practices and reviews past performances, a work team must review past actions, learn from mistakes, plan new strategies, and build up team morale and spirit. Any manager now needs to be able to form teams quickly and establish an atmosphere conducive to productive working relationships.

Both existing and newly formed teams are faced with the same tasks:

- Building relationships.
- Creating a positive working atmosphere.
- Establishing agreed working procedures.

In helping a team to function effectively we need to provide the following:

- Clear roles for the team itself and the individual members.
- The generation of an informal working atmosphere.
- Effective control of time whilst the team is working.
- Periodic assessments of team performance.
- Rewards for performance that are commensurate with efforts.
- Organisational recognition of the team's performances and contributions.
- Acceptance and implementation of the team's work.

Team development

Key Management Concept

A classic approach to team development was formulated by Bruce Tuckman in the 1960's and updated in the 1970's. It is regarded as a definitive approach to understanding how teams grow and develop and is based on four sequential stages of development:

1. Forming
2. Storming

3. Norming

4. Performing

His model suggests that as managers we need to guide our teams through these different phases, and he suggests a range of advice to assist us in understanding our role as team leaders.

The Classic Team Development Cycle

FORMING	STORMING	NORMING	PERFORMING
• Impersonal	• Losing team members	• Developing skills	• Tolerance
• Guarded	• Difficulties	• Getting organised	• Open
• Polite	• Opting out	• Systems established	• Flexible
• Watchful	• Confronting	• Task focus	• Maturity
	• Managing conflicts	• Confronting issues	• Sharing
	• Feeling stuck	• Agreed procedures	• Energy

Testing ⟶ Infighting ⟶ Sharing and Doing ➤ Performing

Source: BW Tuckman

Forming

(Newness, Honeymoon, Impersonal)

Behavioural characteristics of this team stage:

- Politeness.

- Superficiality.

- Avoid controversy.

- Suspense – what's going to happen to me?

- Withholding of information.

- Watchful of other members.

- Relatively low levels of involvement and participation.

- Fear, anxiety, nervousness.

The team leadership issues:

- Dependence on the leader.

- Providing direction: moving the team from the comfort of non-threatening topics to encountering the risk of conflict.

Team and people issues:

- Inclusion – will I be included?

- What will happen to me?

- Who are these people?

- Am I going to enjoy this?

Tactics to help a team move through this phase:

- Establish a clear direction and goals.

- Identify the resources available to the team.

- Effect introductions.

- Build a supportive atmosphere.

- Identify relevant parties outside the team.

- Clarify individual roles, expectations and objectives.

- Get the team doing things together.

Storming

(Challenge, Conflict, Competition, Difficulties)

Behavioural characteristics of this team stage:

- Feeling stuck: 'what we supposed to be doing?'

- Feeling expressed as 'I'm fed up with this'.

- Opting out.

- Resistance to requests.

- Competitive behaviour between team members.

- Sub-groups developing.

- Jockeying for position – who's in charge here?

- Differences are expressed openly.

The team leadership issues:

- People drop out.

- Loss of impetus.

- Counter-dependence on the leader plus resistance.

Team and people issues:

- The search for control and influence.

- Leadership of the team.

- Sense of frustration and loss of direction.

Tactics to help a team move through this phase:

- Define and re-define the team leadership role.

- Clarify the decision making processes.

- Clarify roles, responsibilities and expectations.

- Promote real listening.

- Establish procedures and team processes.

- Provide positive feedback.

- Manage the conflict constructively – identify the issues.

- Stay relaxed and calm – see this stage as natural and positive.

- Move the team from 'testing and proving' to a 'problem solving mentality'.

Norming

(Maturing, Sharing, Getting down to business)

Behavioural characteristics of this team stage:

- Give and take amongst team members.

- Acceptance and agreement on roles and responsibilities.

- Procedures and processes understood by all.

- Ground rules for meetings are set and understood.

- Decision-making generated from discussion.

- Increased levels of active listening.

The team leadership issues:

- Interdependence of members and leader.

- Sharing and completing work together.

Team and people issues:

- Support and acceptance of others.

- Sharing of feelings and ideas.

- Soliciting and giving feedback to each other.

- Creativity increasing.

- Openness.

- Feeling good about being part of the team.

Tactics to help a team move through this phase:

- Demonstrate 'give and take'.

- Discuss team dynamics.

- Ask for input versus telling.

- Focus on team goals and objectives when conflicts arise.

- Demonstrate openness to feedback.

- Re-clarify roles and responsibilities.

- Confront issues.

Performing

(Unity, Confidence, Maturity, High Energy)

Behavioural characteristics of this team stage:

- High performance and productivity through problem solving and work.

- Strong mutual support and co-operation.

- Giving and getting feedback.

- Lots of emotional and task support evident in team working.

- Follow through on action plans.

- Team identity, spirit, pride, cohesion.

- All members contribute.

- Flexibility in outlook and approach.

- Compliance is replaced by commitment.

The team leadership issues:

- Interdependence of the team and leader.

- Role of the leader – redundancy?!

Team and people issues:

- Caring.

- Risk-taking .

- Trust and support.

Tactics to help a team move through this phase:

- Delegate, coach and develop team members.

- Enhance openness .

- Promote supportive and creative confrontation of ideas.

- Seek out feedback

- Let go!

How to start up a team building process

To effectively start up an initial team building session we need to think about four steps.

1 Establishing the purpose and objectives for the team

Team members can often have different levels of commitment or priority to a team or project, and to avoid later conflicts it is a good idea to:

- Detail the fundamental purpose and objectives for formulating the team.

- Get each team member to contribute their thoughts about the goals or task.

- Ask each team member to explain their current priorities and assignments.

- Ask each team member how much time they can commit to the team's priorities. It is better to resolve potential conflict about availability now.

- Have the team determine a realistic timetable for completing the work. Where appropriate allow those who can commit more time to accept more responsibility.

2 Share concerns and expectations

Discussing team member concerns and making them part of a team building agenda helps ensure positive teamwork. Try to allow individuals five minutes to prepare responses to the following questions:

- What are your biggest concerns about working on this project and team?

- How would this team function if it was working at maximum performance?

- What are the potential barriers to developing a high performance team?

- What specific actions do we need to take to ensure that we operate as a high performance team?

3 Clarify goals

Team goals need to be set to unify the team and provide direction for its work. In discussing the team goals members will need to:

- Agree on the central goal and aim of the team.

- Evaluate all proposed plans and strategies against the central goals.

- Determine timescales for the team's work.

4 Develop operating guidelines

Any team needs to establish guidelines for operating. Team members need to be clear as to any procedures or rules for working. The team will therefore need to decide:

- How decisions will be made – by consensus, the team leader or the individual responsible for the task?

- How the work will be assessed and reviewed.

- How individual concerns will be discussed – review meetings or one to one sessions?

- How differences will be resolved – majority vote or leader decision?

- How revisions to plans in the face of under performance will take place.

Once your team building session has been completed and you have agreed these various operating guidelines your team will be ready to begin working.

A strategy for day to day teamworking

Listed below is a model for operating effective teamwork on a day to day basis. As a model it can be taken as a checklist against which your team can plan, implement and evaluate its activities by:

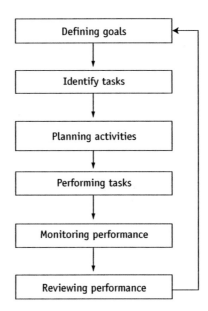

Defining goals

Whatever the task facing your team, it is essential that you establish clearly defined goals. Of course when setting any goals you must be realistic about the timescales involved and your team's ability and capacity to achieve them.

A typical error in goal setting

A sales team sets demanding sales goals for a trading period. In time these goals prove overly ambitious and unrealistic such that the team subsequently fails to meet them. This then disrupts financial plans and in turn production schedules. Initially the team responds by increasing activity and exerting extra effort. Repeated failure to attain the goals however results in a loss of morale and in some cases a team crisis.

But whilst most teams can become too ambitious when setting objectives, other teams can set goals that are too low. In these instances the team goals are always exceeded and as a result they produce a lack of challenge or drive in the team's performance.

Without clear and realistic performance criteria a goal is intangible and any team will have difficulties in achieving them. Consequently any motivational impact will be reduced. The message is that all goals have to realistic if they are to generate effective individual and team performance.

Another important task involves making the team goals explicit so as to avoid people making dangerous assumptions. How many times have we heard comments during team meetings such as 'We don't need to waste time discussing why we are here. Let's get on with it, time is short!' Goals which are implicit rather than explicit often result in team members pursuing activities with aims that are different to those that have been jointly agreed or discussed. The usual signs of a team working with unclear goals are running disagreements during the course of a project, or chaos in the later stages as people struggle to fit together their various inputs into a framework that is obviously not clear to everyone.

Identifying tasks

Having defined and agreed our team's goals we need to define the key tasks necessary to achieve them. These tasks will either be a series of inter-related and sequential activities or a collection of tasks that need to be performed concurrently.

A typical error in identifying tasks

After identifying the first key tasks the team then moves straight into action without necessarily identifying the other tasks that may be critical to the overall project. This inevitably creates confusion as the team continuously moves from identifying tasks to implementing them and back again.

Planning activities

Planning involves allocating time and team members and resources to each key task. At this stage team organisation is critical and as managers or team leaders we need to address the following questions:

- Focusing on the goals, the identified tasks and the resources available to the team, what is the most effective and efficient way of organising ourselves?

- Is it necessary to have a formal leader? If yes, then what should the leader's role be: to provide technical input, co-ordinate team members' activities and inputs, or provide a platform of ideas?

A typical error in planning is that the team can become too absorbed in the activity such that they forget about the pressures and need for implementation. You cannot plan forever. Sooner or later you have to take action to deliver results and a careful balance has to be made between planning and taking action.

Executing new and additional tasks

As a team's tasks are completed the need to perform additional tasks may be apparent as projects seldom occur within a vacuum. At this stage it may be necessary to re-plan, since any new or additional tasks may require additional resources and a re-organisation of project priorities.

Key Question

Reviewing performance

Reviewing performance

At the end of any project we need to examine the team's performance, **not** in terms of the tasks, but in terms of its goals or outputs. The key questions to ask ourselves are:

- Did we achieve our goals?

- If so, what did we do well?

- What could we do differently next time?

- If we failed to achieve our goals why?

- Were the goals realistic?

- Were there other factors that prevented us from delivering?

- Did we spend sufficient time planning?

- Were the right tasks identified in our planning?

- Did we adequately project manage the plan?

- Were the tasks performed to the correct level?

- How well did the team work together?

Reviewing these sorts of questions will help any team to learn and revise its approach and processes for the next project. To improve team performance, it is critical to identify any reasons for failure, as well as any reasons for success. A characteristic of high performance teams is that they do take time out to review their working methods and processes as well as the actual results they achieve, whether they were successful or not. Too often in organisations we spend time running on to the next problem or task without necessarily having learnt from the last one.

Team working – processes

There are a large number of observations that can be made on the processes involved in teamwork. Process involves the 'How' of working together and looks at relationships and communications within a team. Process explores how feelings and disagreements are aired within a team. As with running on to the next task most teams take little time to explore how well the process aspects of their team-working functioned. Listed below is a checklist of typical process issues facing a team and their leader; it can be used as a means to monitor team performance or as a simple checklist.

At the same time Fig 10 provides a sample list of process characteristics that result from high performance teams.

Activity

Team effectiveness rating: how does your team rate?

	Fully Effective				Ineffective
	5	4	3	2	1

- Informal atmosphere
- Full participation in discussion
- Task understood and accepted by all
- Members listen to each other
- Team resolves disagreements
- Consensus decision making
- Frequent and frank criticism
- Expression of feelings
- Action planned and commitment given
- Leadership shifts – manager does not dominate
- Team is self conscious about its operation

Action Checklist

Crucial process issues facing any team leader

Issues	Questions
The working atmosphere and relationships	What kind of team relationships are required for success? How close, friendly, formal or informal should they be?
Participation levels	How much participation is required of the team? Some more than others? All equally? Are some members needed more than others? Do we really need to be a team?

Team objectives and commitment	How much do the team members need to understand the goals? How much do they need to accept or be committed to the goals?
Communication and information flows	How is the team to share information? Who needs to know what? Who should listen most to whom?
Conflict management	How should disagreements or conflicts be handled? To what extent should they be resolved?
Decision making processes	How should decisions be made? Consensus? Voting? One-person rule?
Performance evaluation	How is the team's evaluation to be managed? Everyone appraises everyone else? A few take the responsibility? Is it to be avoided?
Role and task assignments	How are role and task assignments to be made? Voluntarily? By team discussion? By the team leader?
Team leadership	Who should lead the team? How should the leadership functions be exercised? Shared? Elected? Appointed from outside?
Process management	How should the team monitor and improve its process management? Ongoing feedback from members? Formal procedures?

Recognising why teams fail

The manager's fault

Manager does not:

- Have a clear and compelling vision.

- Set a clear direction with priorities.

- Hold people accountable for their performance.

- Display appropriate supporting behaviours.

- Allocate resources effectively.

- Build the right team atmosphere.

- Hold effective team meetings.

- Share information with people when they need it.

- Deal with negative team behaviours that conflict with the goals and objectives.

- Understand people's feelings.

- Understand what is really going on in the organisation.

- Develop people or their potential.

- Manage the interface between the team and the rest of the organisation.

- Like feedback from team members.

The team's fault

Team members do not:

- Recognise the critical issues and the necessity for change.

- Take responsibility for their contributions.

- Recognise their interdependence in reaching their goals (they are competitive as opposed to collaborative in their behaviour).

- Possess basic interpersonal skills.

- Confront conflicts, and prefer to choose scapegoats outside of the team to blame.

- Develop the technical competence for their position.

- Take responsibility for their part in follow-on action plans.

- Deal with the real issues in the team.

- Put team goals above self-interest.

- Deal with each other on the basis of 'personality problems' versus problem solving to achieve organisational goals.

- Understand the business they are in.

- Participate fully in the team process.

Understanding your team roles

Key Management Concept

Belbin's team preferences

Through his extensive research Meredith Belbin has devised a world recognised method of identifying team preferences which help us to understand why people will behave in certain ways in teams. He identified eight types of preference for working in teams, and below are highlighted some of the essential characteristics of each type:

- Company Worker/Implementor

- Chair/Co-ordinator
- Shaper
- Plant
- Resource Investigator
- Monitor Evaluator
- Team Worker
- Completer Finisher

Belbin's Team Types

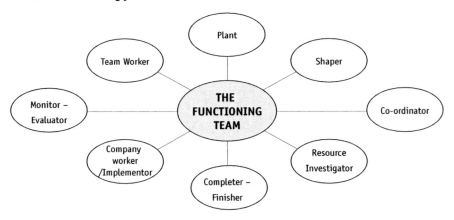

1. The company worker/implementor

Role

- Translates general ideas and plans into practical working objectives.

- Gets down to action.

- Breaks things into tasks and actions.

- Delivers actions and results.

Methods

- Helps ensure that the team's objectives have been properly established and that any tasks have been clearly defined.

- Clarifies any practical details and deals with them.

- Maintains a steady, systematic approach.

- Is calm under pressure and reliable.

- Perseveres in the face of difficult and challenging targets.

- Provides practical support to other team members.

Behaviours to avoid

- Unconstructive criticism of other team members' ideas and suggestions.

- Lack of flexibility. Company workers have a high efficiency concern which means they question the introduction of the 'new'.

- Being resistant to new ideas or innovations.

As a manager, a Company Worker or Implementor's strengths are their ability to define objectives and practical details. They are also very effective in introducing and maintaining procedures and structures. In organisations they are often promoted because of their inherent organising abilities and skills.

2. The co-ordinator/chair

Role

- Controls and organises the activities of the team, making best use of the resources available.

- Pulls the team together.

- Stands back and helicopters above the team.

- Is able to get people working together.

Methods

- Encourages team members to achieve the team's objectives by helping them identify their roles and contributions.

- Encourages people to put the team's objectives before their own.

- Provides positive feedback on individual performance.

- Smoothes over disagreements and inter-team competition with keen people insight and understanding. Uses tact and diplomacy to control and manage.

- Identifies weaknesses in the team's composition and organises and develops the team to neutralise any weaknesses.

- Co-ordinates resources.

- Exercises self-discipline and perseverance. Acts as a focal point for the team's effort, especially when under pressure.

- Delegates effectively.

Behaviours to avoid

- Not recognising the full capabilities of the team. Not using all of the team's resources.

- Competing with other team types.

- Failing to add a creative, innovative or challenging aspect to their role.

- Abdicating the leadership role in the face of strong competition (particularly from Shapers and possibly Plants).

As a manager, a Chair or Co-ordinator is in a good position to lead the team. They are comfortable standing back from the detail and can mobilise people to tackle the issues. Their effective interpersonal skills also mean that people will listen and take their lead from an effective Chair.

3. The shaper

Role

- Makes things happen.

- Gives shape and strong direction to the team's activities.

- Injects energy and drive into a team's proceedings.

Methods

- Directs the team's focus, setting objectives and clear priorities.

- Adopts a wide perspective of the team's goals and helps individuals understand their roles and contributions.

- Exerts a strong directive influence on the team's discussions.

- Summarises outcomes in terms of objectives and targets.

- Will often appear impatient and in a rush.

- Focuses on progress and achievements. Intervenes when the team wanders from their objectives.

- Challenges others if they are pursuing another direction.

- Can be argumentative and dismissive of people who do not move as fast.

Behaviours to avoid

- An overly directive style that assumes undue authority.

- Being too directive in making summaries, appraisals or interventions.

- Not being tactful. Avoid being overly blunt or even rude and insensitive to the needs of others.

- Becoming isolated or remote from the team. Losing identity as a team member. Being seen as too egotistic.

- Competing with other team members, particularly the Plant and the Monitor Evaluator.

A Shaper performs best when operating in a team of peers. If they find themselves in a formal leadership position they may well need to adopt more Co-ordinator type behaviours. This may require more involvement in routine activities and more self-discipline. Shapers normally focus on a broad brush approach to getting things done. They have little time for the detail and want to drive forward. They also need to watch that their insensitivity to the needs of others does not in the long term create problems for them. Tact and diplomacy is not always a high priority for shapers.

4. The plant

Role

- Acts as a primary source of ideas and innovation for the team.
- Creative – an 'agent provocateur'.
- An independent perspective.

Methods

- Concentrates their attention on the big issues and major strategies.
- Formulates new and often radical ideas and approaches.
- Looks for possible breakthroughs in approaches and methods.
- Times their contributions; presenting proposals at appropriate moments.

Behaviours to avoid

- Attempting to demonstrate their capabilities over too wide a field.
- Contributing ideas for reasons of self interest and indulgence rather than the team's needs, and so alienating the team.
- Taking offence when their ideas are evaluated, criticised and possibly rejected. Sulking and refusing to make any further contributions to the team.
- Becoming too inhibited about putting ideas forward, especially in dominant, extrovert, or over-critical groups. Being intimidated or alternatively arguing with Shapers.

A Plant needs to exercise self-discipline and be prepared to listen to team members' comments on their ideas and proposals (particularly their Monitor Evaluator colleague(s)). If found in a leadership role a Plant must not let the stresses of controlling the team stifle their creative input.

In non-directive roles a Plant should expect to be used as a strong team resource; devoting their energies and talents towards establishing their role as a creative thinker and ideas person.

5. The resource investigator

Role

- Explores the team's outside resources and develops useful contacts for the team.

- Harnesses resources for the team.

- A networker and free agent.

Methods

- Makes excellent contacts quickly. Develops effective and useful relationships and allies for the team.

- Uses their interest in new ideas and approaches to explore outside possibilities. Introduces new people and resources to the team.

- Develops their role as the team's main point of contact with outside groups. Keeps up to date with new and related developments that may be helpful to the team's work.

- Helps maintain good relationships in the team and encourages team members to make best use of their talents, especially when the team is under pressure.

Behaviours to avoid

- Becoming too involved with their own ideas at the expense of exploring others.
- Rejecting ideas or information before submitting them to the team.
- Relaxing too much when the pressure is off.
- Getting involved in wasteful or unproductive activities. This often results from the resource investigator's natural sociability.

Resource Investigators are skilled communicators with a creative outlook. They are vital to helping bring new resources into a team and their networking capabilities make them invaluable.

6. The monitor evaluator

Role

- Analyses ideas and suggestions.
- Evaluates ideas and approaches for their feasibility and practical value.
- Deals with facts.
- Introduces a high level of critical thinking ability to any team.

Methods

- Uses high levels of critical thinking ability to assess issues and plans.

- Balances an experimenting outlook with a critical assessment.

- Builds on others' suggestions or ideas. Helps the team to turn ideas into practical applications.

- Makes firm but practical and realistic arguments against the adoption of unsound approaches to problems.

- Is diplomatic when challenging suggestions.

Behaviours to avoid

- Using their critical thinking ability at the team's expense.

- Tactless and destructive criticism of colleagues' suggestions. Liable to upset others because of this.

- Negative thinking; allowing critical thinking skills to outweigh their openness to new ideas. Provoking a 'You always see reasons why it cannot be done!' type of response.

- Competitive behaviour with others.

- Lowering the team's morale by being excessively critical and objective.

A successful Monitor Evaluator combines high critical thinking skills with a practical outlook. When a Monitor Evaluator is a team leader they need to ensure that they do not dominate other members of the team and stifle contributions. When in a non-directive role a Monitor Evaluator has the challenge of making their voice heard and not appearing threatening to colleagues. If they can avoid a tendency towards undue scepticism and cynicism their strengths will help them develop their management capability.

7. The team worker

Role

- Strong team player.
- Helps individual team members to contribute.
- Promotes and maintains team spirit and effectiveness.

Methods

- Applies themselves to the task.
- Observes the strengths and weaknesses of team members.
- Supports team members in developing their strengths, eg builds on suggestions and contributions.
- Helps individuals manage their weaknesses with personal advice and assistance.
- Selfless in outlook.
- Improves team communications and builds relationships.
- Fosters a strong sense of team spirit by setting an example.

Behaviours to avoid

- Competing for status or control in the team.
- Aligning with one team member against another.
- Avoiding resolving conflict situations.
- Delaying tough decisions.

The team worker role can be exercised at different levels within a team. As a manager the Team Worker should see their role as a delegator and developer of people. Team Worker's qualities of conscientiousness and perseverance will help ensure that projects are completed on time, and to the necessary levels of cost and quality. But they have to watch that their sense of duty in wanting to help team members achieve objectives often overrides their concerns for task or goal achievements.

8. The completer finisher

Role

- Ensures all the team's efforts are as near perfect as possible.

- Ensures that tasks are completed and that nothing is overlooked.

- Injects urgency into problems and projects that fall behind.

- Provides attention to detail.

Methods

- Perfectionist – looks for errors or omissions; especially those that may result from unclear responsibilities.

- Works on tasks where attention to detail and precision are important.

- Looks for mistakes in detail.

- Actively identifies work or tasks that require more detailed attention.

- Raises the standards of all the team's activities.

- Maintains a sense of urgency and priority.

Behaviours to avoid

- Unnecessary emphasis on detail at the expense of the overall plan and direction.

- Negative thinking or destructive criticism.

- Lowering team morale by excessive worrying.

- Appearing slow moving or lacking in enthusiasm.

A Completer Finisher role can be exercised at different levels within a team and can be easily combined with another role. As a manager a Completer Finisher needs to pay careful attention to their delegation skills and to keep unnecessary interference to a minimum. In a junior role a Completer Finisher will need to develop tact and discretion so as to avoid earning a reputation as a 'nit picker and worrier'. Completer Finishers also tend to possess a nervous drive that needs to be controlled and directed if it is to have positive results.

The following page provides a summary of the various characteristics of the Belbin Types.

Belbin team types summary

Type	Typical features	Positive qualities	Allowable weaknesses
Company worker/ implementor	Solid, dependable, predicable and reliable	Organising ability, practical common sense, hard working, self discipline	Lack of flexibility, unresponsiveness to unproven ideas. Concern to maintain the status quo on efficiency
Chair/ co-ordinator	Steady, patient, self confident, controlled, commands respect	Puts people at ease. Able to get people working together. Good at standing back. A strong sense of objectives and task achievements	Not necessarily the best at thinking radically or creatively
Type	Typical features	Positive qualities	Allowable weaknesses
Shaper	Energetic, outgoing, tense, dynamic, egotistic	Drive and readiness to make things happen. Challenges ineffectiveness, complacency or self-deception	Prone to provoca-tion, irritation and impatience. Can be selfish in terms of satisfying self first

Plant	Individualistic, serious-minded, unorthodox	Genius, imagination, intellect, knowledge. Concerned with the Big Issues	Up in the clouds, inclined to disregard practical details or protocol. Wrapped up with own ideas
Resource investigator	Extroverted, enthusiastic, curious, communicative	A capacity for contacting people and exploring anything new. An ability to respond to challenges and harness resources. Able to sell ideas and excite people	Liable to lose interest once the initial fascination has passed. Needs to be kept focused
Monitor evaluator	Unemotional, cautious, rational and analytical	Judgement, discretion, hard-headedness. Does things right	Lacks inspiration or the ability to activate others. Over concerned with getting things right

Type	Typical features	Positive qualities	Allowable weaknesses
Team worker	Interpersonally skilled, sensitive, strong team player	An ability to respond to people and to situations, and to promote team spirit	Indecisiveness at moments of crisis. Being too kind to others or over anxious about individuals
Completer finisher	Detail oriented, conscientious, anxious	A capacity for follow through. Perfectionist. Creates urgency, provides focus	A tendency to worry about small things. A reluctance to 'let go'. Can annoy by excessive worrying

Key actions

- Consider your role preferences?
- How do they impact on your effectiveness?
- Think of your colleagues and their preferences?
- Review your team's composition?
- Consider the tasks your team has to perform?

Mastering time management

Chapter 8

Managing our time effectively

Most of us like to project an image of being busy and hardworking but too frequently we fail to examine the results of all our activity. At the same time many of us complain about not having enough time to do things. This is because we fail to manage the time we have effectively. Frequently we fail to focus on our priorities and allow less important activities to distract us. As a result the urgent short term issues drive out our important, strategic issues. Many of us might respond to these comments by arguing that our time management problems are often the fault of other people's behaviour; constant interruptions; lengthy meetings; overly complex reporting requirements and so on. Whilst there maybe some truth in these factors good managers can overcome them. By simple analysis, planning and self discipline we are all capable of saving a considerable amount of wasted time each day. This means managing and redirecting our time to more focused and planned purposes.

In managing our time we should consider two main elements:

1 Our routine time

This is the time we use to manage our day to day activities eg administration, meeting staff.

2 Our defensible time

This is the time we use for dealing with our real priorities, eg thinking, strategic planning, budgeting, customer meetings.

Action point

Delegation

Delegate anything that other people can do:

- **Better than you.** Are you taking advantage of people who have more knowledge and experience of you in aspects of your role?

- **At less cost than you.** Are you using your time effectively given what you earn? Are there other people who could do the work at a lower cost to your organisation?

- **As part of their development and training.** If you are having to do something that you think someone else should be doing, then you may well have identified a training need for that person. Use the situation to develop their skills and capabilities.

- **As part of their normal work load.** Is it possible to pass activities on to other people as part of their day to day activities? Are you holding on to things that other people could do?

Remember to delegate authority as well as responsibility and resist the temptation to hang on to all the interesting jobs yourself.

Questions for analysing your use of time.

Managing your time effectively

Be clear about your objectives

- Are you allocating sufficient attention to your current activities, reviewing past performance and future planning? In particular are you devoting sufficient time to planning for the future?

- Are you allocating your time correctly between different aspects of your job? Are there any parts of your job on which you are spending too much time?

- Who are the people you ought to be allocating time to? Are you spending sufficient time with them?

Consider your work

- Do you organise your working day and week according to your priorities? Or do you deal with problems as and when they occur without stopping to think if there is something more important that you should be focusing on?

- Are you able to complete tasks uninterrupted or are you constantly interrupted? Are the interruptions an essential part of your work or part of your own making?

- Are you certain that you are not working on tasks or issues that you could delegate? Remember many people say they could do more if they were only allowed to by their managers.

Try considering the following as potential targets for managing your time. How possible would it be for you to achieve them?

- Reduce your working week by 10 hours.

- Reduce daily interruptions by 50 per cent.

- Reduce the time you spend on phone calls by 50 per cent.

- Reduce the time you spend on e-mail and correspondence by 30 per cent.

- Double the time you allocate to planning and thinking.

- Allocate at least 30 minutes each day for quality thinking.

Tackling 'time robbers'

A time robber is something that prevents us from completing more important and productive tasks. Time robbers are activities that absorb lots of time without producing equivalent benefit for the efforts employed. Interruptions, lengthy meetings and routine tasks (that could be delegated), are some of the most common time robbers we have to face. To control time robbers we need to employ techniques such as avoiding the activity, shortening the time we spend on it, or simply eliminating it altogether. The following is a list of classic time robbers. Review the list and highlight those you have difficulty with.

	Big problem for me	Often a problem	Seldom a problem
Planning and organising			
1 Not setting SMART objectives			
2 Failing to plan on a daily basis			
3 Unclear or changing priorities			
4 Leaving tasks unfinished			
5 Crisis Management – too much 'fire fighting'			
6 Poor self-discipline			

	Big problem for me	Often a problem	Seldom a problem
Planning and organising			
7 Over-stretching myself – setting unrealistic targets			
8 Lack of organisation/ untidy desk – too much paperwork			
9 Lack of clear responsibility and authority			
10 Too many people reporting to me or that I have to report to			
11 Doing too much myself			
12 Getting too involved in routine detail			
13 Poor delegation skills			
14 Lacking motivation to do anything about it			
15 Inability to say 'no' to others			
16 Not coping with change			
17 Telephone interruptions			
18 Casual visitors			
19 My self-discipline			
20 Too many interests			
21 Mistakes			
22 Failing to maintain standards, progress reports			
23 Incomplete information			

	Big problem for me	Often a problem	Seldom a problem
Communicating			
24 Effectively stating my objectives at meetings			
25 Under/unclear/ over-communicating			
26 Failing to listen properly			
27 Socialising too frequently			
Decision-making			
28 Snap decision-making			
29 Indecision/delay			
30 Decision by committee			
31 Perfectionist tendencies			

Managing your time more effectively

1   Keep focused on your personal objectives.

2   In order not to delay or put off decisions

- deal with one task at a time

- allocate specific times of the day for key activities eg making important phone calls – call between 10.00 – 10.30 each day

- keep to your plans

- begin NOW, TODAY!

Action Checklist

Understanding your motivation.

3   Don't destroy your good ideas with negative talk. Think results and outcomes. Stay focused – this will help you motivate yourself on difficult tasks and avoid those that are unnecessary.

4   Work smarter not harder – spend more time on the important issues, less on the urgent.

5   Don't work in panic mode and wait until the last minute.

6   Review your working practices regularly – should you really be doing the jobs that you are.

7   Find time to do your Big Picture thinking – to be creative.

8   Do you sometimes feel weak? Is this a fact or fear? Again, avoid negativity.

9   Set time-scales for completing all tasks.

10   Indulge yourself, make time for breaks and undertake pleasant tasks on a regular basis, find time for your interests and hobbies.

11   Begin the day with an early success, then you are in right frame of mind to tackle the day's challenges.

12   Instigate BANJO immediately – Bang A Nasty Job Off, every day.

Time management challenges and ideas

Classic problem	Response
Personal interruptions	• Begin a process of red time appointments: no interruptions • Work in a quiet room • Operate an engaged 'keep out' notice

Telephone interruptions	• State you have 'one minute only' • Request they call back • Say 'Sorry it's not convenient at the moment' or 'I can give you five minutes'
Personal organisation	• Establish clear goals • Be clear as to your key result areas • Focus on your key objectives • Buy a time management organiser • Read a book on time management
Paperwork overload	• Use the 4 'D's: Delegate, Deal, Destroy, Divert
Waiting action	• Operate a time fillers file – deal with the issues in slack moments
Never enough hours in the day	• Delegate tasks, say' NO' more often • Operate a rigorous 'To-do' list
Disorganised desk	• Operate a 'Musts', 'Shoulds' and 'Coulds' filing system • Review your in-tray twice a day – be ruthless in dealing with paper
Too many crises	• Ask why are they happening?
Meetings too long	• Operate a 60/90 minute rule • Get people to submit proposals in advance

Action Checklist

*Planning and organising
your time.*

On a daily basis

1 Plan tomorrow today
   - list all the things you need to do
   - value each task, prioritise them
   - complete certain tasks together, eg telephoning, dictating, reading
   - calculate the time for each activity
   - allocate parts of the day to deal with each group of tasks.

2 Leave part of your day free to deal with the unexpected.

3 Highlight one major objective for the day and complete it.

4 Think about what is your best time for working: complete important tasks during this period.

5 Reduce interruptions.

6 Plan a reflective 'thinking' period for part of your day.

7 Review your daily plans.

8 Remember you cannot influence the length of the working day.

9 Travel by train, it is preferable to car journeys. You can work on the way and arrive fresh.

10 Which of the following activities do you feel uncomfortable about doing?
   - sitting and thinking, however important?
   - sitting and reading, however relevant?
   - having a clear desk, however effective?

11 Do the above activities generate results? If they do why should you feel guilty?

Dealing with office interruptions

1 Be clear as to what is more important, the task in hand or the interruption.

2 Don't get trapped by detail – take control of the interruption, set up a separate meeting, ask them to come back.

3 Ask your assistant to screen visitors.

4 Train your staff to say 'Is now a good time?' as they interrupt.

5 Specify a set time for the interruption and keep to it ('I can give you five minutes!').

6 Get people to submit a list of points in advance when they ask for an appointment so that your time is not wasted on irrelevant matters.

7 Use another office for 'thinking' or important creative work.

8 Don't be afraid to offend, say 'no' more often ('Sorry I have another urgent appointment').

9 Suggest that someone else meets the visitor.

10 Remain standing up: sitting down can lead to the interruption becoming a meeting.

11 Whilst an open door policy represents a positive attitude it should not be interpreted literally for every minute of the day.

12 Be honest with time-wasters. ('I'm sorry I don't have the time to deal with this at the moment').

Action Checklist

Minimise the effects of interruptions.

How to reduce crises

1 Use effective diary planning to pre-empt problems.

2 Be decisive, don't leave things to the last minute.

Action Checklist

Managing crises.

3   Focus on your key objectives: don't get side tracked by urgent but relatively unimportant tasks or problems.

4   Remember that things normally take longer than you think: allow for this when planning.

5   What do you want to achieve? What are your expectations?
   • what will happen if you stay as you are?
   • what are all the steps required?
   • what is the first step?
   • start today!

6   Problem solving:
   • first define the problem, not the answer
   • emphasise your key objectives in addressing the problem
   • list all the possible solutions: be radical and creative in your thinking
   • identify the available resources
   • select the most suitable solution
   • implement your solution
   • review the results.

Operating a clean desk policy

Action Checklist

Ensuring that efficient time management is maintained.

1   Keep only relevant papers on your desk: the task you are currently dealing with.

2   Let other people know that you are operating a clean desk policy.

3   Deal with all papers immediately using the following guidelines:
   • action it (80% of paperwork can be dealt with immediately)
   • identify the main points and then bin or file.

4   Clear your desk at the end of each day.

5   Record actions in your diary rather than a desk file to remind you of important tasks.

6   Complete each small task before moving to another.

7   Take action sooner rather than later.

8   Use pocket dictators, word processors and hand written notes for speed.

9   Do your own filing.

10   Try to touch a piece of paper only once.

Mastering meetings

Chapter 9

Managing meetings

Meetings can be a very effective means of communicating, but all too frequently we get insufficient benefit from them because we spend too much time in meetings relative to the results we achieve. This is because we often focus discussions too much on what has to be achieved rather than how best to achieve the actions or results. To run successful meetings we need to be concerned with both of these dimensions. Whilst it is vital that people are clear about what it is they have to achieve they also need to be clear as to how they are going to achieve it. Remember people attending any meeting are there to achieve an objective or purpose. When chairing meetings we need to ensure that everyone is clear about aims and objectives and that everyone attending the meeting contributes fully to the discussions.

We also need to be absolutely clear as to whether the meeting's objective is to discuss issues, develop alternatives, approve plans, agree actions or develop people's commitment. Without this information any meeting runs the risk of wandering into unproductive time.

Guide to Best Practice

Techniques for managing meetings.

The process side of meetings

The skills needed to successfully run meetings involve encouraging people to contribute and at the same time controlling the discussions to keep proceedings on track. The following behaviours can help you to achieve these aims.

Behaviours to encourage individual contributions during a meeting

When chairing meetings make sure you:

- Use open ended questions that collect information.

- Use direct eye contact with the group or specific individuals.

- Highlight people's expertise and encourage or invite their comments.

- Give people notice that you want them to speak. eg mention their name, followed by a preamble, followed by an open question. ' I know

Pierre has a view on this following his experiences with x, Pierre perhaps you would like to share your views with us?'

- Use silences to provoke input – if you stay quiet someone will eventually break the silence.

- Manage a formal sequence of contributions: ask people one after each other to comment. This stops people cross talking and puts them on alert.

- Test understanding of issues by summarising and asking for comments.

- Build on people's suggestions or ideas: help create a positive climate.

- Increase the formality level of the meeting, eg all comments through the chair please.

Behaviours to avoid in chairing meetings

- Interrupting other people.

- Shutting out people by ignoring them.

- Defending or attacking people; as a chairperson you need to be objective. If we have too strong views on a subject we should get someone else to run the meeting.

- Allowing sub meetings to break out: only one person at a time should speak.

- Making judgmental comments; to avoid such behaviours ask others for their opinions before you comment.

Controlling the direction of meetings

To control the direction of a meeting use the following approaches:

- Allocate specific times to each agenda item.

- Announce how you plan to run the meeting at the beginning. This helps set expectations.

- Use short open-ended questions to help guide the discussions.

- Make regular summaries, followed by open-ended questions on any new subject areas that need to be explored.

- Use direct questions towards people who meander in their comments.

Changing the pace of meetings

Your opening statement will influence the pace of any meeting. A long and slowly delivered introduction will set the tone for a slow meeting, whilst a fast paced and focused introduction is likely to be followed by a faster moving and more effective meeting.

Review progress during the meeting to help create more energy and increase the pace. Try 'How do people feel we are progressing – do we need to move faster?'

Closed questions will tend to speed up a meeting, whereas summaries slow down proceedings.

You can also inject more energy into a meeting by being more animated, and putting more variation in your voice tone or by speaking faster.

Successful meetings are ones that not only achieve objectives but do so in an effective way. As a chairperson it is your function to achieve results using the most appropriate process. You can use a wide range of behaviours to achieve this. The above lists give some of the more commonly used behaviours. With such a wide range of behaviours available to help you direct your meetings it is possible to successfully run them without using the more formal powers of the chair's role.

Action points A quick guide to a chairperson's role

- Make plenty of positive suggestions.
- Try to build on people's ideas.
- Summarise regularly.
- Manage rather than avoid conflicts.
- Listen, listen, listen.
- Use eye contact.
- Watch for non-verbal behaviours.
- Be conscious of the impact of the hygiene factor eg seats, heatings.

Why meetings go wrong

- Poorly defined objectives or aim.
- Not being clear as to the outcomes that need to be achieved.
- Bad control exercised by the chairperson.
- Insufficient time to achieve the objectives set.
- No clear agenda.
- Disruptive behaviours allowed to flourish.
- The wrong people attending (because of protocol or office politics rather than need).
- Too many people attending.
- Failure to address the real issues: too much game playing around the real problems.
- Poor environment: room too hot, inadequate seating, interruptions.

Controlling forceful or dominant characters in a meeting

In any meeting we will at sometime or other need to manage strong or forceful characters. Taking control is the sign of an effective chair and the strategies listed below can help you manage difficult people.

- Ask the individual closed questions so as to prevent them giving protracted answers or making speeches. For example 'So can you simply confirm your agreement or not?'

- Breaking eye contact with someone can indicate that you want to move onto other people.

- By using outward hand gestures you can signal that you want the person to conclude their comments or observations. This can be enforced by a tactful comment such as 'Thank you for that contribution Jean' as you signal.

- Interrupting and skilfully summarising what they have said can control proceedings and at the same time inject speed.

- Introduce greater formality: if you anticipate a noisy meeting introducing a more formal tone can help you control proceedings. The use of formal titles can raise the sense of formality eg 'Mr. Johnson, I'd like to ask a question'.

- Switching the conversation to other team members, either by directed questions (in response to appropriate body language) or by shifting eye contact.

Managing the classic disruptive characters at meetings

The Football Terrace Supporter

Likes to attack and antagonise others. Aggressive in approach and voice tone.

Tactics: appeal to the rest of the group – isolate them. Institutionalise the role: say it's helpful as devil's advocate.

The Expert

Likes to help but keeps interrupting with explanations or lots of detail.

Tactics: appeal to their innate nature – can you help me? Carry out a specific role during the meeting. Take a note of issues we miss or fail to recognise.

The Introvert

Says nothing, stays removed from the proceedings even though their input is necessary.

Comment tactfully to the whole group that 'quiet' people get a lot from meetings without necessarily speaking or contributing. This will concentrate them on trying to contribute to avoid being labelled as shy or quiet.

The Detail Freak

Likes to promote themselves as guardians of wisdom or truth.

Likes to concentrate on details and point out inconsistencies when the group is moving forward.

Tactics: point out the need to simplify issues for preliminary discussion then record all their comments. Discuss their issues during recess and ask for advice on how to address them. Get them to recite points to the reconvened meeting.

The Doodler

The potential day dreamer.

Don't intervene, but if distracting, again try to harness their inputs by direct questions.

The Passive Interrupter

Generates side-discussions with colleagues so leading to disruptive behaviour. Intervene, 'Is there a problem or issue?' 'Anything you want to share with the rest of the group?'

How to make your meetings more productive

- Ask yourself is the meeting really necessary? Are there other ways in which you could achieve your objectives? What could you be doing instead?

- What are your objectives in holding the meeting:
  - To make a decision
  - To communicate key plans or new developments
  - To review progress on an issue
  - To generate new ideas (brainstorming type sessions)
  - To develop a consensus.

- Produce an agenda with clear objectives.

- An ideal meeting time duration is 10 – 50 minutes.

- Ideal time after 11.00 am.

- Keep the number attending as small as possible. The ideal number of participants is seven.

- Communicate the meeting's objectives, time and location to participants.

- If necessary, be clear that you ask people to prepare or bring information to the meeting in advance. Make sure you also provide adequate notice.

- Start the meeting on time and finish on time.

- Get to the point: start with what's important.

- Keep to the agenda: we all like our meetings to be managed strongly.

- Encourage people to leave the meeting when their involvement is no longer required.

- Use presentational aids to encourage interest and participation.

- Prevent interruptions from other people.

- If you find a meeting to be slow in pace so will others, so advise the chair.

- As the chairperson, summarise at key stages and signpost where the proceedings are going to move on to.

- Avoid 'Any other business' sections as they are usually a substitute for poor preparation.

- Question whether you need to get into the game of taking elaborate minutes or notes. They are often a substitute for 'Cover your arse!' type cultures. A simple decision or action sheet is much more useful.

- Should your meetings be held standing up?

Mastering the skills of assertion

Chapter 10

The difference between passive, assertive and aggressive behaviour

Passive behaviour

Passive behaviour is often described as being apathetic or unresponsive. Passive behaviour does not allow someone to assert their rights and can be characterised by an 'I lose you win' perspective . This results in an individual feeling that they have been either victimised or perhaps landed the rough end of a deal.

In contrast, aggressive behaviour involves being threatening and domineering and frequently results in a 'I win, you lose' scenario. People who are passive or unassertive can fall victim to aggressive behaviour, so in trying to combat such tactics it is important to understand why someone might be using aggressive behaviours.

Aggressive behaviour often involves putting someone down though the use of anger and hurt. Ridicule or humiliation is also another component of aggressive behaviour. Why would someone use such behaviour? Well there are many possible reasons such as:

- A simple lack of knowledge of other effective influencing behaviours. 'I only know how to get things done by shouting at people!'.

- A genuine lack of human insight and sensitivity towards others. They simply do not realise the impact of their behaviour, or if they do they choose to ignore it. In which case they may be an uncaring and selfish individual.

- An inflated and egotistical personality can often result in unreasonable behaviours. 'I am right and you are wrong so there.'

- A feeling of powerlessness and low self esteem. In some cases extremely aggressive behaviour can be the result of an individual's own negative feelings about themselves. Their lack of a positive self-image causes them to hide behind an aggressive exterior which they may mistakenly confuse with appearing strong and confident.

- A fear of being threatened by someone else. 'By getting my retaliation in first I am being strong.'

- Past experiences can cause some people to react aggressively. In situations where they may have been exposed or feel weakened they may want to again assert their rights by aggressive behaviour or demands.

The consequences of aggressive behaviour can be:

- A sense of satisfaction from the immediate release and assertion that the person is in control. 'I told them who was boss today. Nobody was left in no doubt who was in charge!'

- A sense of achievement in terms of satisfying short–term needs. 'I really screwed them on the price to get the deal I wanted.'

- Retaliation in the long run. People who are on the end of aggressive behaviour normally resort to finding ways in which they can get their own back in the long–term: even if it does take a long time.

- Defensiveness on the part of the individual. Aggressive behaviour normally restricts rather than promotes dialogue between two people, such that the individual may appear to always be on the defensive.

- Sub-optimal results. In the long–run aggressive behaviour will always be reciprocated and that invariably means that it generates results that fall short of what could have been achieved by other means.

Assertive behaviour

Assertive behaviour is a major approach to enhancing our influencing skills. Assertion skills are based on some fundamental principles. These principles are often referred to as the Bill of Rights and they form the building blocks of assertive behaviour:

- I have a right to exist.

- I have a right to state my own needs and wants.

- I have the right to be treated with respect.

- I have the right to express my own feelings, values and opinions.

- I have the right to say yes or no for myself.

- I have the right to make mistakes.

- I have the right to change my own mind.

- I have the right to say I do not understand.

- I have the right to decline responsibility for other people's problems.

- I have the right to deal with others without having to depend on their approval.

These principles in turn have implications for how we need to deal with other people. These can be best expressed by the following statements:

- Everybody has their own personal space.
- We do not have the right to invade another person's space without invitation.
- We do not have the right to manipulate others.
- Other people have the choice as to whether or not they want to respond to us.

Assertive people try to be authentic in their dealings with others and always try to be rational. They also seek to 'own' the problem they are dealing with and not push it onto someone else. Assertive people are also not afraid to express their feelings and emotions to persuade or influence other people. So assertive behaviour enables someone to express their needs in simple but direct terms, whereby the emphasis is on respecting others and being fair to oneself.

The consequences of assertive behaviour are:

- A greater sense of self-respect and individual identity.

- Increased self confidence.

- Greater mental and physical well being: reduced stress and anxiety at work.

- Optimisation of your performance potential.

Behaving assertively

Assertive behaviours demand that we:

- Tell other people what we want.

- Protect our needs and avoid being manipulated by others by seeking clarification of other people's requests.

- Confront problems as soon as possible.

Guide to Best Practice

Assertiveness techniques

Use 'I' statements and avoid the use of 'We', 'One', and 'You'. The use of 'I' is much more forceful than hiding behind the company or the boss or the team. When you want something 'I' is much more influential.

At the same time keep your comments and statements short and to the point. Avoid the tendency in difficult situations to over elaborate which often provides people with other cues to latch onto.

If the discussions get heated always remain calm and keep your voice tone low and moderated.

Assertive behaviour recognises some basic rights that we all have. Assertive behaviour is also a way of viewing the world that allows you to be persuasive but resistant to manipulation. It is not a manipulation technique but simply a skill that allows you to express yourself more openly and forcefully. In learning some of the skills of assertive behaviour we need to accept the existence of these basic rights.

Using assertive techniques in giving feedback

Different types of assertive behaviour have been developed and one important approach involves giving feedback to other people. Giving assertive feedback focuses on three critical areas:

- The specific behaviour under discussion.

- The expression of feelings surrounding a situation.

- The impact of the behaviour under discussion.

The specific behaviour under discussion

This should be a clear statement of the behaviour that has generated the problem. When commenting you need to be specific and avoid any generalisations or judgments about the behaviour. Simply refer to the observed behaviour.

'We agreed that during the negotiations with the customer we would stick to the existing pricing policy and you ignored that agreement half way through the meeting without discussing it with me!'

The expression of feelings surrounding a situation

In many work situations the expression of personal feelings is often thought to be a sign of weakness or a lack of professionalism. This is a flawed perspective as the forceful expression of feelings can have a powerful impact on other people. Assertive people are comfortable in expressing their feelings as a way of asserting their needs. For example, I am very angry, irritated, annoyed that you did not deliver as we had previously agreed'

Of course in order to express our feelings we need to identify what precise feelings have been aroused by a particular behaviour. There is no point in simply reacting in a hysterical manner. So we need to be clear what has happened and why it has impacted on us in a particular way before we commit.

Expressing our feelings and emotions can also help reduce our stress levels since it prevents us 'storing up' negative thoughts and worries. Conversely when we analyse our feelings we may find out that we are in fact over-reacting and that we can actually live with the behaviour.

The impact of the behaviour under discussion

When talking to someone about the impact of their behaviour on us we need to be more concerned with the specific impact rather than the 'possibilities or risks' associated with the behaviour. This vital distinction can help us to identify the specific sources of our annoyance with greater precision and so possibly prevent us from over reacting. No matter how well a message is presented to someone it often causes an emotional reaction.

As well as giving feedback assertive behaviour also helps us in coping with feedback from other people. When facing difficult or aggressive situations we can all react emotionally. Whilst some of us will 'fight back' and escalate the problem others will accept the feedback passively and without asserting our viewpoint.

Fogging

Fogging is a technique that enables us to receive negative feedback without necessarily agreeing with the comments being made. By avoiding overly emotional reactions we are in a better position to gather the available feedback so that we can evaluate it and at a later stage, preferably when alone and in a less emotionally charged atmosphere, decide how we want to respond to it.

Typical phrases which employ fogging might include:

'I can see that'

'I can understand that'

'I can see you're upset about this'

'I can see why that would annoy you'

'I can accept that'.

The purpose of such statements are to express acceptance and understanding of the other point of view, without necessarily accepting responsibility for the cause or any possible solution.

Of course in certain situations the feedback given to us may not be intended to be useful, but may be simply designed to provoke an emotional reaction. When facing these types of situations we can use some of the following techniques:

Negative assertion

This technique involves using specific but open-ended questions to identify the exact nature of the feedback that is being given to you. It forces the giver to identify exactly the specific behaviour that has caused the problem.

'So you think the work is rubbish! Could you help me understand what it is precisely about the work that makes you think it is rubbish?'

Exhausting the criticism

This technique uses a lengthy list of open-ended questions to exhaust the negative feedback or complaints.

'Is there anything else about the work you don't like?'

'I understand that issue, is there anything else that you want to add or say?'

Negative assertion is not intended as a way of rejecting feedback but rather a way of dealing with ineffective feedback by converting it into more useful and helpful messages that you can act on. By asking for or stimulating constructive criticism you help others to express any honest and negative feelings directly to you and so improve communication between you. This will also expose any manipulative or invalid criticisms.

A quick guide to developing assertiveness skills

Action Checklist

Using the techniques of negative inquiry

- **Turn the attention on yourself, not your critic.** By using expressions such as 'What is it about me that's wrong' you avoid focusing on your critic, which often generates a defensive reaction that then escalates rather than improves a situation. So draw the feedback to yourself and don't react to the individual but use their energy to get them to focus on you. Drain them of their negative energy by simply absorbing it.

Key Learning Point

- **Invite criticism or feedback.** You will extract feelings from others more effectively if you convey the message, 'I'm very eager to hear this valuable information. I want to know more. What don't you like about my approach?'

- **Identify the specific comments or observations surrounding any criticism.** Listen closely to the words being used and help your critic focus on exactly what is wrong.

  Q 'You say this report is rubbish? What is it about the report that is rubbish?'

  A 'Well, your structure, for one thing'.

  Q 'What is it about my structure that is rubbish?'

  A 'Well just look at it. You haven't listed the key conclusions.'

  Q 'Then it's my conclusions not being clearly defined that makes the report look rubbish?'

  Q 'OK – that's one thing.'

- **Exhaust the criticism.**

  Q 'Is there anything else about my report that is wrong?' Or, 'There must be more things about the report that is wrong than just my conclusion'. Or, 'Are you sure there's nothing else that's wrong with the report?'

- **Analyse the criticism.**

  Q 'What is it about .... that's wrong?'

- **Listen for the 'I' statement.** Remember that criticism often comes from someone else's value system, that they are often unaware that their subjective value system is operating, and that behind every piece of criticism is a statement that 'I don't like it.'

- **Specify what your critic wants.** You might make unwarranted assumptions if you don't do this.

  Q 'It sounds like you want me to clear things with you before I submit my report?'

  A 'Yes ..... Well no. Go ahead and make the decision. Just be sure to let me know as soon as possible. It's when I don't know that you've done it that I have problems.'

You now have more information on which to act and manage this person.

Admitting to mistakes without beating yourself up

Often we attack ourselves for making errors. To avoid this we need to accept valid criticism without letting it escalate. Non-assertive people cope with mistakes but they can be manipulated by others through feelings of guilt or anxiety. The result is that they:

- Repeatedly seek forgiveness for making mistakes and try to make up for them.

- Alternatively, they deny the error by being defensive and engage in counter criticism, which provides hostile critics with a target on which to work out their aggressive feelings or frustration.

In either case the non-assertive person copes poorly and ultimately feels worse.

As with most of the beliefs we learned in childhood, few of us can actively change our belief that errors make us feel guilty by simply thinking about it. We must first change the way we behave and what we say to ourselves when dealing with an error so that we can react more positively to any criticism.

So how, then, do you cope assertively with errors? The easiest way is to is to simply view them as errors, no more or less, errors are just errors. In other words, you assertively accept which errors are negative about yourself. For example, when you are confronted with a critical or possibly hostile comment when making an error you can assertively accept the fact of the error by saying:

'I've forgotten to bring the keys to let us in – what a stupid mistake. What's the best thing to do now?'

This approach stops you getting into lengthy justifications as to how it was you came to forget the keys and more importantly, focuses on how you can best solve the difficulty. Other examples might entail statements such as:

'I'm sorry, I did not make a very good job of that report, you're quite right.'

'I'm afraid it simply slipped my memory, I'm sorry it has made it so difficult for you, would it help if I ....'.

'I hadn't realised I kept interrupting you, I know it's a really annoying habit – I'll try to be more aware of what I'm doing in the future.'

By agreeing with and accepting valid criticism, you acknowledge your mistake. Remembering that you have a right to make mistakes without accepting any generalised accusations or sweeping judgements of your personality. Thus you maintain your self-esteem.

Using the broken record technique

Once you are clear about what you want, be prepared to repeat your need over and over again. This will help you to maintain your position in the face of manipulative comments, irrelevant logic or argumentative comments.

'Yes I realise your other commitments but as we previously agreed I must have the report tomorrow morning at 9.30pm. Yes I realise the difficulties but I have to have the report at 9.30. Tomorrow morning at 9.30!'

By simply repeating your need – like a broken record – and not over elaborating or siding with the other person's needs they will soon accept your requirement.

The fogging technique

Fogging as we have already discussed is a technique that enables you to absorb another person's views, anger or hostility without reacting in any other way that simply acknowledging what they are saying. In effect you give them nothing back to escalate the anger or debate. This is a particularly useful technique in situations where we may want to simply let the other person get the issue off their chest.

Fogging might sound like:

- Yes I can see why you are annoyed.

- I fully appreciate how you feel.

- I quite understand your anger.

By acknowledging what the other person is saying without responding specifically you can maintain your own needs without feeling defensive, aggressive or anxious. Fogging means not giving the other person something back to get further annoyed or angry.

Dealing with unjust criticism

Quite often if we are criticised by someone we develop feelings of guilt or insecurity. We may become defensive and begin to make excuses or we may involve ourselves in an argument which gets us nowhere.

By using the fogging technique and some other rules we can also deal with manipulative criticism, as it enables us to have a defence against those who may try to influence us to behave in a certain way by using unjust criticism. By using this technique we can create situations which make it impossible for the other person to have any success. It should of course not be used where any criticism is valid. Whilst acknowledging that there may be some truth in what someone says, you essentially remain your own judge of what you do as a result. Thus this approach allows you to receive criticism without becoming anxious or defensive, while giving no rewards to those attempting to apply manipulative criticism.

In addition to the use of fogging the technique involves applying a few other simple rules:

- **Do not deny any criticism** – if you do you are providing the other person with more ammunition.

- **Do not become defensive** – if you do you are admitting that the criticism may be justified.

- **Do not respond by counter criticism** – this may escalate matters and start an argument.

- **DO LISTEN** – and respond using the same words.

- **Respond ONLY to what the critic actually says, not to what they imply.**

Examples of statements that can be employed are:

- 'You may be right.'

- 'I can understand why you think that.'

- 'That's a point. You obviously feel strongly about the matter.'

Calling time out

Calling time out is a simple but powerful technique that allows you to buy time to think about a situation and respond in a more considered manner at a later time. Often we can be put into a difficult situation by people almost jumping on us and demanding an immediate response. This often puts us off guard and what assertive people are good at is finding the time to gather their thoughts in a controlled manner. The response can be a simple

'I understand that you have to deal with an angry customer, however, at this exact moment in time I do not have all the background or information to respond properly. If you can let me have ten to fifteen minutes then I will get back to you on these points'.

You will observe that the response is very considered and reasonable. It acknowledges the person's plight and gives a real commitment to respond in a set time. Of course this might vary depending on the circumstances from a few minutes to one week. But often people rely on us dropping everything to deal with their issues regardless of our needs. Calling time out is a simple way of asserting your rights to get the right information in order to respond. It can be very effective in dealing with people who barge into your office demanding immediate satisfaction. It can also help in dealing with irate customers. Clearly however you must get back to people otherwise you will have an even bigger problem when they return. Again assertiveness involves commitments on your behalf. It is NOT a technique for getting rid of difficult tasks.

Engage in self-disclosure

If you offer information about yourself without feeling self-conscious, you encourage others to feel more at ease and therefore more able to share what is important or difficult for them to express.

Learning to say 'No!'

We all find ourselves in situations where we maybe trying to make a point but the other person seems intent on avoiding or ignoring our request or refusal. When another person fails to accept your refusal or request and resorts to pressure tactics you need to handle the situation in a more assertive way. We do this by simply choosing a phrase or statement that we feel comfortable with, and without getting angry or loud we simply repeat the statement each time the other person tries another form of manipulation to persuade you to change your mind.

By staying focused on our statement and resisting the temptation to answer, or respond to attacks or insults, we can eventually convince the other person that we are not prepared to be ignored or diverted, for example:

'I can't work late this evening.'

'I don't think you heard me, I'm not able to work this evening.'

'Let me say it again, I'm not able to work this evening.'

'That's really irrelevant to the main issue, which is that I'm not able to work this evening'.

This broken record use of the assertive 'No' will eventually get heard as it is uncomfortable to listen to for too long. It really is an effective way of saying 'No' in difficult situations and can provide you with a greater sense of confidence and so deal with anxiety .

Using empathy

When saying 'no' to people we need to be careful that there is no confusion between refusing a request and rejecting the person. Some people fall into this trap and confuse a 'No' as a rejection of them. By employing empathy with people we can soften the 'No' side of any refusal.

This is easily achieved by simply reflecting back to the other person their request but adding 'I'm sorry, I can't do that'. This helps to show that you have listened to the request and that you do empathise, for example 'I really understand your problem about completing the work urgently but I'm not able to work this evening because of a previous commitment'. We are in effect trying to sympathise with the other person's difficulty but at the same time asserting our needs. Whereas a flat no can send a more aggressive message of 'I don't care' which may not be effective for developing long term relationships.

Promote workable compromises

This technique often needs to be combined with the 'how to say No ' technique. On hearing of the 'Broken Record, No' Technique some people will rightly argue that wandering around their organisation flatly refusing to help people will result in their swift exit from the organisation – and they are probably right. So it is important to realise that assertiveness is not about behaving in an uncooperative way or manner. A key part of assertiveness skills involves seeking alternative options or compromises.

If someone won't give in and is being equally assertive with you it is often appropriate to offer a compromise to both parties. (Remembering that your goals include self-respect, not necessarily getting your own way and defending yourself, rather than allowing yourself to be put down). When your self respect is not in question try offering a compromise that may work for both parties for example 'I can't work late this evening but as it is important, I'm prepared to come in early tomorrow'.

In most situations we can manage the situation more effectively by better using the 'How to say no' technique along with empathy and a genuine willingness to look for a workable compromise. Assertiveness is not about rejecting people, it involves a requirement on the individual to seek out satisfactory outcomes for both parties.

Eight essential tips in behaving assertively

1 Never hit below the belt

Blows below the belt are unfair. We all have certain areas that are sensitive to us and that if breached we cannot be expected to respond rationally. The effect of hitting below the belt is to cause hurt and resentment and puts any working relationship in danger. Such strategies are normally the domain of the bully.

2 Don't play games

Don't pretend to go along with something or agree to it when you don't. Equally don't pretend to be something you are not. Stay true to yourself and be honest in your dealings with others. Assertiveness is about being authentic and genuine.

3 Don't play the amateur psychologist

None of us have the ability to read the mind of another person. All the information we have about people involves what we can see in terms of their behaviour. Nothing angers someone more than telling them what they are 'really' thinking, or what they are 'really' like, and what is causing their behaviour. So stick to commenting on what people do and not what you think they are thinking!

4 Avoid stereotyping

No one likes being boxed or labelled. We all want to be regarded as individuals. Stereotyping someone has the potential to cause resentment. Deal with people as individuals and avoid labelling them as types. For example, cone heads, digit heads etc.

5 Avoid 'piggy-banking'

Don't let minor grievances pass without comment until you have a whole piggy-bank full of them. The danger is that one 'last straw' mistake may cause your full piggy-bank to burst, creating a spilling out of all past resentments and making a huge issue out a small one. If someone does something that annoys you deal with it promptly – don't save it for a rainy day.

6 Forget the past and work on the future

Don't live in the past and dig into history. The past cannot be changed – it can only be learnt from. Try to focus on the future and work in the 'here and now'.

7 Avoid generalisations

Generalising statements about people such as 'You always..' or 'You never..' are pointless and accomplish little. Assertive behaviour demands that we are specific about the comments we make of others.

8 Don't go ballistic

Do not use techniques of overkill. Do not threaten extreme sanctions for minor mistakes or errors. In over reacting to situations you only weaken your credibility and case.

Neutralising anger

In angry situations we may well need to try to reduce our feelings of aggression so that we:

- Feel more comfortable.

- Begin to listen.

- Can begin to try to solve the problem together.

When someone is criticising us or is involved in a personal attack against us and we want to confront the problem rather than escape, fight, or pretend there is not a problem, then it is important to neutralise feelings of anger. We might consider using the following technique with a boss, friend, colleague, or any other person in authority who is engaged in attacking.

The action steps for neutralising anger

1 Recognise the anger being displayed:
   'I can see you are very angry.'

2 Express your desire to solve the problem(s):
   'I want to hear what you have to say. Let's try and work this out together.'

3 Get the angry person to lower their voice and sit down by using a normal voice and a calming tone:
   'Why don't you sit down and see if we can talk about what's happened. I really want to go through this issue.'

4 Use the skills of active listening to hear all the complaints before moving into any problem-solving mode:
   'It sounds like this has been irritating you for a long time. This last incident must have seemed like the end.'

In some situations it can help to admit early on the possibility that you might have been part of the problem:

'May be I could have arrived earlier.'

'I want to hear what you have to say. Perhaps I made a mistake.'

This way of approaching anger naturally assumes we are willing to handle the problem and move beyond active listening to try to resolve the problem. if we are simply trying to placate the other person this may well lead to further conflict. We have to be serious about solving the issue.

Summary
checklists

Chapter 11

Are you a leader or a ****

Leader	****
Carries things for people	Hovers over the problems
Appeals to the best in people; opens doors; provides guidance and is a cheerleader	Is anonymous and invisible – expects instructions to be carried out without question
Thinks of ways to empower people to greater productive and rewards, is focused on company goals	Thinks of personal rewards, status and how they look to outsiders
At ease with people – values them	Uncomfortable/strained – uses people
Removes parking places and other executive privileges	Has them in abundance – actively encourages them
Goes where people want	Sits where they want
Good listener	Good talker
Simplistic on company values	Good at demonstrating their command of all business complexities
Available	Hard to reach
Firm but fair	Fair to favoured few; exploits the rest

Decisive and has conviction	Uses committees, bureaucracy
Ego in place	Egotistic and arrogant in equal amounts
Tough – confronts nasty problems head on	Elusive – the artful dodger – looks for other fall guys
Persistent	Only when something of value is at stake
Simplifies (makes it look easy)	Complicates (makes it look difficult)
Tolerant of open disagreement / conflict	Intolerant of open disagreement / conflict
Knows people's names	Doesn't know people's names
Has strong convictions	Vacillates when a decision is needed
Does dog-work when necessary	Above doing any kind of dog-work
Trusts people	Trusts only words and numbers on paper
Delegates whole important jobs	Retains all final decisions
Spends as little time as possible with outside activities except customers	Spends a lot of time massaging own and sometimes customers' interests
Wants anonymity for himself, publicity for his company	Self-serving

Often takes the blame	Looks for a scapegoat
Gives credit to others	Takes all the credit; complains about lack of good people
Gives honest, frequent feedback	Information flows one way – into their office
Knows when and how to fire people	Ducks unpleasant tasks or does them very badly
Goes to help where there is trouble	Interrupts people in crisis and calls them to meetings in their office
Respects all people	Thinks a lot of people are lazy and incompetent
Knows the business and the kind of people who make it tick	They've never met
Honest under pressure	Two faced – says one thing does another
Looks to abolish controls	Loves introducing new controls
Prefers face to face contact instead of memos	Prefers memos, long reports, written communication
Straightforward	Tricky, manipulative
Consistent and credible to people	Unpredictable; says what they think people want to hear

Admits own mistakes; comforts others when they admit them	Allegedly never makes mistakes; blames others; starts witch hunts to identify culprits
No policy manuals	Policy manuals
Openness	Secrecy

How is management in your organisation?

(Adapted from an idea originally contained in Tom Peters and Nancy Austins' 'A Passion For Excellence', Collins 1985.)

Absolute don'ts for real leaders

1 Don't abuse people.

2 Don't make people feel weak.

3 Don't talk at people all the time.

4 Don't devalue people or simply 'use' them.

5 Don't deny responsibility.

6 Don't avoid risk.

7 Don't avoid people problems.

8 Don't gloss over issues.

9 Don't de-motivate.

10 Don't be negative.

11 Don't be reactive.

12 Don't be lazy.

13 Don't always insist on perfection.

14 Don't resist change.

15 Don't be pessimistic.

16 Don't tell lies.

17 Don't be indecisive.

18 Don't lose sight of your goals / aims.

19 Don't be inconsistent.

Listening

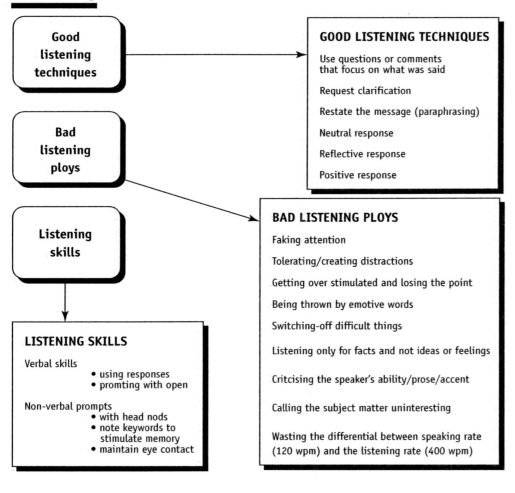

Good listening techniques

Bad listening ploys

Listening skills

GOOD LISTENING TECHNIQUES

Use questions or comments
that focus on what was said

Request clarification

Restate the message (paraphrasing)

Neutral response

Reflective response

Positive response

BAD LISTENING PLOYS

Faking attention

Tolerating/creating distractions

Getting over stimulated and losing the point

Being thrown by emotive words

Switching-off difficult things

Listening only for facts and not ideas or feelings

Critcising the speaker's ability/prose/accent

Calling the subject matter uninteresting

Wasting the differential between speaking rate
(120 wpm) and the listening rate (400 wpm)

LISTENING SKILLS

Verbal skills
- using responses
- promting with open

Non-verbal prompts
- with head nods
- note keywords to
  stimulate memory
- maintain eye contact

Feedback

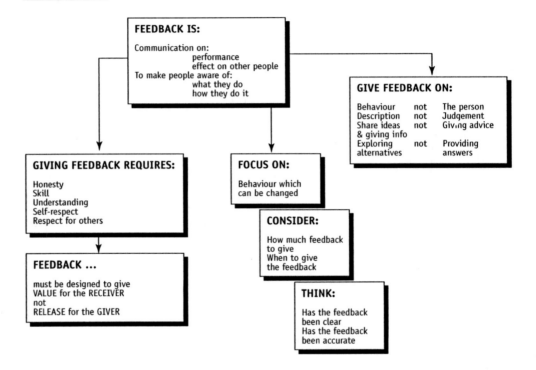

FEEDBACK IS:

Communication on:
   performance
   effect on other people
To make people aware of:
   what they do
   how they do it

GIVE FEEDBACK ON:

Behaviour	not	The person
Description	not	Judgement
Share ideas	not	Giving advice
& giving info		
Exploring	not	Providing
alternatives		answers

GIVING FEEDBACK REQUIRES:

Honesty
Skill
Understanding
Self-respect
Respect for others

FOCUS ON:

Behaviour which
can be changed

CONSIDER:

How much feedback
to give
When to give
the feedback

FEEDBACK ...

must be designed to give
VALUE for the RECEIVER
not
RELEASE for the GIVER

THINK:

Has the feedback
been clear
Has the feedback
been accurate

Delegation

What is delegation?

Delegation varies in degree from 'instruction' to 'abdication'.

Delegation can be defined as:

'Giving someone the freedom and authority to handle certain matters on their own initiative – with the confidence that they can do the job successfully.'

How should you delegate?

Before delegation	• Select the right staff.	
	• Train and develop them.	
	• Plan what is to be delegated.	
When delegating	• Tell them	– what is to be done
		– why it has to be done
		– what results required and when
		– what authority has been given.
	• Tell others	– what authority has been given.
When the job is being done	• Check progress at agreed stages.	
	• Help only if asked.	
After the job	• Give constructive feedback.	

What can and cannot be delegated?

Delegate	• Routine jobs and decision making if
	  – team members can do them
	  – better
	  – quicker
	  – more cheaply.
	  – they can help develop team members.

Don't delegate	• People development reviews. • Assessing individual results. • Communicating to the team. • Planning and setting individual objectives.

A simple guide to managing performance

Key results areas	Performance standards
1	
2	
3	
4	
5	
6	
7	

Objectives to be achieved	Action steps to achieve objectives
Area of responsibility: *(Use key action verbs)* Objective: Target Date:	
Area of responsibility: Objective: Target Date:	
Area of responsibility: Objective: Target Date:	
Area of responsibility: Objective: Target Date:	
Personal development area: Objective:	

A short guide to making better use of your time

Ask yourself these questions

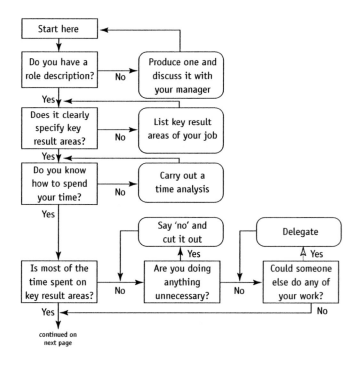

continued on
next page

High performing team checklist

This checklist is designed to help you think about the behaviour in your team. Read over the scales and place a cross on the scale that typifies the behaviour of your team.

1. Listening to others

Low   High

2. Participation by group members

Low   High

3. Building of decision making

Low   High

4. Building and developing on others' contributions

Low   High

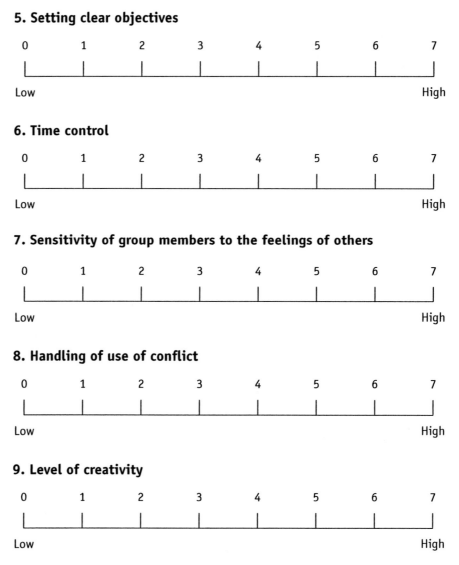

5. Setting clear objectives

| 0 | 1 | 2 | 3 | 4 | 5 | 6 | 7 |

Low   High

6. Time control

| 0 | 1 | 2 | 3 | 4 | 5 | 6 | 7 |

Low   High

7. Sensitivity of group members to the feelings of others

| 0 | 1 | 2 | 3 | 4 | 5 | 6 | 7 |

Low   High

8. Handling of use of conflict

| 0 | 1 | 2 | 3 | 4 | 5 | 6 | 7 |

Low   High

9. Level of creativity

| 0 | 1 | 2 | 3 | 4 | 5 | 6 | 7 |

Low   High

Consider the effectiveness of your team.

The key rules of assertiveness

- Prepare what you want to say
- Know what you want
- Ask for it
- Accept the risk element involved in being assertive
- Stay calm
- Express your feelings openly
- Give and accept praise without embarrassment
- Give and accept fair and constructive criticism
- Use the minimum amount of assertiveness to achieve your objective
- Do not ramble on – be succinct
- Do not be devious or manipulative
- Do not threaten or bully
- Do not bottle up your feelings
- Preserve people's integrity and dignity

Listening skills checklist

Here are some practical measures to help you become a better listener:

- Listen carefully to the actual words being said

- Occasionally ask for clarification, check your understanding

- Reflect feelings and facts back to the speaker

- Observe the speaker's body language

- Don't let your emotions cloud your perception

- Let the speakers finish, avoid interrupting

- Nod, look interested

- Maintain eye contact

- Lean forward

- Say 'Uh, uh'...'yes'...'I see'

- Reserve judgement

- Summarise from time to time

- Don't switch off

- Don't drift onto another line of thought

- Demonstrate respect, be courteous

- Empathise with the speaker

- Use sympathetic body language

NOTES

Thorogood publishing

Thorogood publishes a wide range of books, reports, special briefings, psychometric tests and videos. Listed below is a selection of key titles.

Desktop Guides

The marketing strategy desktop guide	*Norton Paley* • £16.99
The sales manager's desktop guide	*Mike Gale and Julian Clay* • £16.99
The company director's desktop guide	*David Martin* • £16.99
The credit controller's desktop guide	*Roger Mason* • £16.99
The company secretary's desktop guide	*Roger Mason* • £16.99
The finance and accountancy desktop guide	*Ralph Tiffin* • £16.99
The commercial engineer's desktop guide	*Tim Boyce* • £16.99
The training manager's desktop guide	*Eddie Davies* • £16.99
The PR practitioner's desktop guide	*Caroline Black* • £16.99
Win new business – the desktop guide	*Susan Croft* • £16.99

Masters in Management

Mastering business planning and strategy	*Paul Elkin* • £19.99
Mastering financial management	*Stephen Brookson* • £19.99
Mastering leadership	*Michael Williams* • £19.99
Mastering marketing	*Ian Ruskin-Brown* • £22.00
Mastering negotiations	*Eric Evans* • £19.99
Mastering people management	*Mark Thomas* • £19.99
Mastering personal and interpersonal skills	*Peter Haddon* • £16.99
Mastering project management	*Cathy Lake* • £19.99

Business Action Pocketbooks

Edited by David Irwin

Building your business pocketbook	£10.99
Developing yourself and your staff pocketbook	£10.99
Finance and profitability pocketbook	£10.99
Managing and employing people pocketbook	£10.99
Sales and marketing pocketbook	£10.99
Managing projects and operations pocketbook	£9.99
Effective business communications pocketbook	£9.99
PR techniques that work	*Edited by Jim Dunn* • £9.99
Adair on leadership	*Edited by Neil Thomas* • £9.99

Other titles

The John Adair handbook of management and leadership	*Edited by Neil Thomas* • £29.95
The inside track to successful management	*Dr Gerald Kushel* • £16.95
The pension trustee's handbook (2nd edition)	*Robin Ellison* • £25
Boost your company's profits	*Barrie Pearson* • £12.99
Negotiate to succeed	*Julie Lewthwaite* • £12.99
The management tool kit	*Sultan Kermally* • £10.99
Working smarter	*Graham Roberts-Phelps* • £15.99
Test your management skills	*Michael Williams* • £12.99
The art of headless chicken management	*Elly Brewer and Mark Edwards* • £6.99
Exploiting IT in business	*David Irwin* • £12.99
EMU challenge and change – the implications for business	*John Atkin* • £11.99
Everything you need for an NVQ in management	*Julie Lewthwaite* • £19.99
Time management and personal development	*John Adair and Melanie Allen* • £9.99

Sales management and organisation	*Peter Green* • £9.99
Telephone tactics	*Graham Roberts-Phelps* • £9.99
Business health check	*Carol O' Connor* • £12.99
Companies don't succeed people do!	*Graham Roberts-Phelps* • £12.99
Inspiring leadership	*John Adair* • £24.99
The book of Me	*Barrie Pearson and Neil Thomas* • £24.99

Thorogood also has an extensive range of reports and special briefings which are written specifically for professionals wanting expert information.

For a full listing of all Thorogood publications, or to order any title, please call Thorogood Customer Services on 020 7749 4748 or fax on 020 7729 6110. Alternatively view our website at **www.thorogood.ws**.